Queen Anne's Lace
Blooms Again

Joyfully yours,

Mary Jane Hartman

Deborah~
  This was written by my
grandmother. I hope you enjoy!
Thank you for everything this year!!
You have been amazing! Fly with Christ~
                                            Amy

Queen Anne's
Lace
Blooms
Again

Mary Jane Hartman

Providence House Publishers
PROVIDENCE PUBLISHING CORPORATION
FRANKLIN, TENNESSEE

To
My special grandchildren,
Amy and Hart Knight

Printed in the United States of America

06   05   04   03   02   1   2   3   4   5

Library of Congress Catalog Card Number: 2002110436

ISBN: 1-57736-280-2

Cover illustration by Elaine Kernea Wilson
Cover design by Lindrel Hobbs

PROVIDENCE HOUSE PUBLISHERS
an imprint of
Providence Publishing Corporation
238 Seaboard Lane • Franklin, Tennessee 37067
www.providencepubcorp.com
800-321-5692

Contents

Foreword

One of my greatest joys in pastoring Brentwood United Methodist Church has been the unique opportunity to develop a pastoral friendship with Mary Jane Hartman. Her gracious spirit, her warm hospitality, and her genuine Christian character, which has been tested in the flames of time, shine from her very being. Physically challenged by every step, Mary Jane continues to walk with her Lord, praising Him all the way home.

Many of us know earth to be crammed with heaven. Few of us, however, take the time to stop and notice. Mary Jane looks and listens. She seeks and sees. She beholds and believes. In so doing, she has been able to find the presence of God in the most unlikely places—yes, even a common weed.

As we peek into life through the eyes and experiences of Mary Jane, we, too, catch a glimpse of the God who is with us even when we do not notice. As she encourages us to be as well as do and to notice as well as knock, she gently leads us into the presence of the One whose grace is always sufficient for every need. As our complexity gives way to simplicity, we find ourselves face to face with the God who fails us not.

Thanks be to God for this gift of insight and inspiration along the daily paths of life!

J. Howard Olds
Senior Pastor
Brentwood United Methodist Church

Preface & Acknowledgments

"He called it just a common weed,
Wild carrot with its wayward seed.
She put it in a lovely vase
And gently named it 'Queen Anne's Lace.'"

More than forty years ago, a dear friend sent me this four line verse. The words in this little verse are not stirring or spectacular, not challenging or inspirational, but when words plant a seed they are powerful!

Little did I realize then how those words would someday add a wonderful new dimension to my life. Radical orthopedic surgery had caused drastic changes in my life. Looking for a new outlet to express my feelings, I found it in writing. And my first book, *Queen Anne's Lace and Other Weeds*, was born.

Here I offer you a new book which I am calling *Queen Anne's Lace Blooms Again* because it is based on the same concepts as the first book. In these brief meditations I have attempted to share some thoughts and words with you in the hope that they will:

- bring you some joy
- give you some comfort
- provide some inspiration
- bring you some peace
- sharpen your awareness of God's beauty around you
- help you sense God's presence in your life.

My hope and prayer is that these words will go where I may never go and bless the lives of people I may never know.

I express my grateful appreciation to an untold number who have helped to shape my life and my beliefs by their example, their encouragement, and their wise counsel.

My early education came from the public school system in a small Iowa town which I attended from kindergarten through high school. Two very special teachers, one in junior high and one in senior high, added much to my literary development. My seventh and eighth grade teacher taught me that diagramming sentences could be fun. My high school teacher of English and composition taught me the power of the written word.

I am grateful to my family and many of my friends who have encouraged me to write this second book. Because I think best with a pen in my hand (rather than a keyboard), my husband, Warren, has typed every word and prepared the computer disks for submission to my publisher. I thank him for his ongoing encouragement as well as his editorial suggestions.

My appreciation also goes to Andrew Miller, Providence House publisher; Kelly Bainbridge, managing editor; Elaine Wilson, artist; and all others on the fine Providence House staff. I am deeply grateful to my pastor, Dr. Howard Olds, who wrote the foreword. I also appreciate the affirming words of my friends whose commendations appear on the cover of this book and in some of the publicity releases.

I also gratefully acknowledge the many written sources upon which I have drawn while writing this book. I have noted those which I could identify and have given them credit. Many of the contributions, thoughts, and ideas of others were filed only in my memory. I also acknowledge those persons whom I can no longer recall.

Finally, my thanks to God who continues to speak to me in the everydayness of life.

Queen Anne's Lace
and Other Weeds

Queen *Anne's* *Lace* and Other *Weeds*

*J*uly is one of my favorite months. It is the season that God has chosen to adorn the roadside and fields with Queen Anne's lace and other weeds.

At least once every summer, we drive out along the country roads and gather Queen Anne's lace, elderberry blossoms, wild daisies, and the lovely fragrant milkweed blossoms.

As I arrange the armload of beauty in a favorite antique container, I feel I am looking at a reflection of my Creator:

- Only God could make such beauty bloom with so much abandonment.
- Only God could enable anything to flourish in such arid, sometimes rocky, and unproductive places.
- Only God could create such regal long-stemmed beauties with minute lacy intricacies.
- Only God could make roadside weeds so beautiful.

God rarely reveals Himself to us in the blazing spectacular things in life. He came to us as a baby in a manger. He has taught us through leaven in a lump, a widow's mite, and a mustard seed. He continues to come to us in the simple beauties of this world, in the everyday routines, and through our relationships with others.

We do not need wealth to buy a ticket to enjoy God's beauties along the roadside. We do not need prestige and fame to be admitted into God's kingdom. We need only to open ourselves to Him and to His will for us. He can take our weedy, wayward lives and transform them into bits of loveliness which are just as beautiful as Queen Anne's lace.

Our Forever God

*T*he sky was cloudless. The morning was hushed and still with only the crashing of the waves of the Gulf of Mexico breaking the silence. Bright sunlight caught the peak of each wave creating dancing diamonds against the horizon. The porpoises frolicked as they came near the shore to feed. As they jumped again and again high above the surface of the water they reminded me of a graceful ballet.

I sat alone on a balcony eleven stories above the white sandy beaches. Nearby, familiar voices in friendly conversation occasionally broke in upon my thoughts.

I was mesmerized by the timeless ongoing scene which stretched out before me. It was the same each day—yesterday, today, and tomorrow. I sensed the presence of our "forever" God who had created this vast expanse of beauty which stretched out as far as my eyes could see. I sensed the presence of a faithful God of order, not a God of whim and fancy. I was reminded that our God is One on Whom we can depend at all times. He is:

- a God who always was,
- a God who always is, and
- a God who always will be.

Our God is the God of every phase of our life. We know He has been our faithful help in the past. He is with us this very moment. Our trust and hope in His standfastness assure us that He will be there for us in the future. God is our faithful friend. God never changes. God is forever! It is so difficult for my finite mind to comprehend this truth about our "forever God."

God, in His infinite wisdom, knew that we could never fully understand who He really is just by observing this world He has created and sustains, so He poured part of Himself into a person like us. This person was Jesus, the Christ, who came to show us what God is really like. He came to teach us about a God Who cares for us, a God Who loves us, and a God Who wants only the best for each one of us.

Henri Nouwen, in one of his writings, has affirmed that God knew us and loved each one of us even before we were conceived. Furthermore, God will love us unconditionally throughout our life and He will love us after we leave this earth.

That is what the Apostle John was trying to tell us when he wrote: "God loved the world so much that He gave His only Son that anyone who believes in Him shall not perish, but have eternal life" (John 3:16, TLB).

What Is In a Name?

When I call my doctor's office, a recorded voice comes on with these instructions:

Press 1 if you are a physician calling.
Press 2 if you want to make a routine appointment.
Press 3 if you need to have a prescription refilled.
Press 4 if you need a referral.
Press 5 if you are sick and need to talk to a nurse.
Press 0 if this is an emergency and you need to talk to a "person."

By the time the message ends, I have almost forgotten the reason for my call. Oh, yes, I remember, I need to have a prescription refilled.

I am often an armchair shopper when I find just the thing I need in one of the interesting catalogs which the mail carrier deposits in our box. After I dial the company's toll-free number a recorded voice comes on the line and says, "All of our operators are currently helping other customers. Your call is very important to us. Please stay on the line and your call will be answered in the order in which it was received."

After a long wait a live operator does answer. She asks for the number in the yellow box on the back of my catalog. Her second request is for the number in the blue box on the back of my catalog. Next, she wants me to confirm the numbers in my address as they appear on her computer. Her next question is, "Are you Mary Jane Hartman?" Finally, she wants to know the number on the credit card I'll be using along with the catalog number of the item I wish to order. Throughout the entire conversation, I sense that my name is of less importance than all the numbers I have given to her.

When we go to pick up our dry cleaning, we are asked for our phone number which we gave to the attendant when we dropped off the clothing to be cleaned. If we want to receive the advertised discount at our grocery store, we must give the cashier the plastic discount tag which has our number on it. Our government identifies us by the all-important social security number. That number is also used to identify my primary health care provider. Our bank has given us an account number which is printed on every check. Almost all of our day-to-day business transactions are accomplished by means of numbers. Thus, we are constantly reminded that almost everything in our society operates and functions within the "numbers game."

Am I just a number? Am I not more than that? A number is such a cold impersonal means of identifying who I really am. I am so thankful that God does not use a number to identify me. He knows my name. He knows your name. My finite mind marvels that I, as such a small part of God's vast creative order, receive the same attention and concern as all of God's other creations. Isaiah confirmed this concept years ago when he wrote: "Fear not, for I have redeemed you; I have called you by name" (Isaiah 43:1b NIV).

Many years ago as a small child, our granddaughter, Amy, taught me a little song she had learned in her church choir.

I'm something special
I'm the only one of my kind.
God gave me a body and
A bright and healthy mind.
He had a special purpose
That He wanted me to find.
So, He made me something special
I'm the only one of my kind.

When each of us was born our parents gave us a special name, not a number. Our name identifies us to one another. God also knows us by our name. We are each unique in His eyes and He compares us to no other person. God knows who we really are, warts and all, and still loves us with an unconditional love.

It is a very humbling thought to me that God created you and me at a certain time and for special purposes. We may call him by His name, "Our Father, who art in heaven," because that is what Jesus taught us. God calls me by my name today and claims me as a beloved child. What is more, we do not have to press a number, be put on hold, or take a number and wait in line to talk with Him. He is always there waiting . . . waiting. . . .

Jessica

For a number of years I served as a receptionist in one of our large local churches. On many Wednesday afternoons Jessica, a three-year-old friend, joined me for an hour while her mother rehearsed with our bell choir. Jessica played with her doll and colored while I answered the phone and took messages for the staff.

Jessica was a precious little girl who bounded in the door with the same enthusiastic greeting every time: "Mrs. Hartman, I've missed you!"

She was a very special little girl who needed lots of hugs and kisses, and she gave lots of hugs and kisses to this Granny who needed them, too. Many years later I still treasure the memory of those happy hours we shared with one another. They remind me that:

- children give their love openly—unreservedly with no thought of return;
- God's agape love is like that, too, gushing forth out of His great heart of love;
- children give their love to us whether we deserve it or not; and
- God loves us unconditionally in spite of who we are or what we do.

Every time a baby is baptized at the altar of our church, we pledge as a congregation that we will assist with the spiritual nurture of the little one by repeating this vow from the Baptismal Covenant of the United Methodist Church:

With God's help we will so order our lives after the example of Christ, that this child, surrounded by steadfast love, may be established in the faith, and confirmed and strengthened in the way that leads to life eternal.

These challenging words were found in an attic on an old sampler:

A hundred years from now—
it will not matter what my bank account was;
the sort of house I lived in;
or the kind of car I drove;
but, the world may be better because
I was important in the life of a child.

Ah, children with their innocence and loveliness—they are truly God's precious "little people." As adults, we are given a special gift when we view the world through the eyes of a little child. Let us preserve the treasures that exist in that whisper of time we call "childhood." As mothers and fathers, grandmothers and grandfathers, aunts and uncles, neighbors and friends, let us give children a listening ear, our attention, and our love. They are truly our blessings for today and our hope for tomorrow.

Our children are the messengers to a time we will not see!

Oh, What a Wonder!

Sidney Poitier, the well-known actor, who gave us new understandings through his roles in such outstanding movies as *Lilies of the Field* and *Guess Who's Coming to Dinner?*, is a very private person. He recently broke the silence in an interview when he shared some of his personal attitudes about those things in life which are important to him. At a mature stage in his life he continues to view life with a sense of wonder. He said, "That is the thing that keeps us going—the sense of wonder in our lives."

Webster gives us these synonyms for the word *wonder*: curiosity; astonishment; to be surprised; to marvel. As I read those definitions my mind took me to those little people who always seem to embody these attitudes— our children. The sense of wonder in their eyes and on their faces is a beautiful sight.

Just now I am thinking of one of my piano students, ten-year-old Mark, who had an unlimited sense of wonder about everything. It was not unusual for him to bring one or more of his treasures for me to see when he came for his piano lesson. They ranged from a pretty stone or even a live insect. One day he reached into his pocket and pulled out a small, but very much alive, squirming frog which he had caught that morning. He began to excitedly point out the frog's physical characteristics. He was full of wonder about the little creature.

Someone wrote about a little girl who walked to and from her school on a daily basis. Although the weather was threatening with dark clouds rolling around in the sky, she still made her daily trek. As the day wore on, winds whipped up and sharp flashes of lightning began to make their zigzag patterns across the sky, followed by loud claps of thunder. The little girl's mother became concerned for her daughter's safety in the gathering electric storm, so she got in her car and drove along the route her daughter would be walking.

Soon she spotted her daughter just ahead. At each flash of lightning and clap of thunder, her daughter would stop, look up at the sky, and smile. Another and still another flash of lightning were each followed quickly by a resounding thunder clap. Every time the little girl would stop, look up into the sky, and smile broadly. Finally, the concerned and puzzled mother pulled alongside and called out to her daughter, "What are you doing? Come get in the car."

The little girl answered, "I'm smiling for God while He keeps taking my picture!"

May every child be encouraged to believe they can touch fireflies, catch a falling star, dance with fairies, and smile when God takes their picture.

Another writer told of a pastor who was making house calls. He knocked repeatedly on the door of a home in the neighborhood, but there was no answer. Finally, a little girl who was about three years old opened the door part way. "Shhh," she said as she put her little finger to her lips. With her other hand she motioned for the pastor to follow her into the house.

Again she whispered, "Shhh, God is here!" At this point her father entered the room and explained that God had just brought her a new baby brother and she believed God was still there. The new baby was not of first importance to the little girl. The wonder of it all was that she knew God had come to their home and to their family and had left her a little brother.

Blessed are we when we can see through the innocent eyes and believe through the trusting heart of child. When we do that, we embrace all the reasons to believe in God and in the fullness of life about us.

I am reminded of the importance that Jesus placed on the children around him. Luke tells us that "people were bringing even infants to Him that He might touch them; but when the disciples saw it, they sternly ordered them not to do it. But Jesus called for them and said, 'Let the little children come to me, and do not stop them; for it is to such as these that the kingdom of God belongs. Truly I tell you, whoever does not receive the kingdom of God as a little child will never enter it'" (Luke 18: 15–17 NRSV).

Wrinkles

*W*e live in a society where the epitome of physical beauty is a pencil-thin shapeless figure and a smooth, flawless "peaches and cream" complexion.

For most of us, this is a very unrealistic and unattainable standard of beauty. Of course, God always wants us to do the best we can with the looks He has given to us. However, striving for that kind of false outward physical beauty is surely not our highest calling.

Today, the elusive "fountain of youth" has become both the god and goddess for many. Millions of dollars are spent each year on fad diets and face-lifts, but these outward efforts never add anything to our inner beauty, nor do they bring the contentment and happiness that God has intended for each of us to experience.

Dr. Lori Hansen, a young plastic surgeon, tells her patients that she can do all sorts of things to make them attractive by the standards of our world. However, she reminds them, that alone will not bring them inner peace unless they allow God to make changes from the inside out. She has said, "What I really want to do for my patients is to help them focus on their unique inner God-given beauty."

Surely, we realize that proper makeup and the right hairstyle do not give a woman that kind of inner beauty. The most radiant woman in any room is the one who is full of life, joy, and experience. The actress Rosalind Russell once observed, " Taking joy into her life is a woman's best cosmetic."

Through the years, our daily living brings many kinds of experiences that change our countenance. There are happy times when the laugh lines in our faces are widened and deepened. There are uncertain times when the worry lines and frowns are borne on our brow. There are times of physical trauma and pain when still other lines are etched deeply into our facial features.

We call these lines wrinkles. I like to think that wrinkles born out of our life experiences are honor badges of life. Norman V. Peale wrote, "Years may wrinkle the skin, but lack of enthusiasm wrinkles the soul."

Two individuals come to mind when I think of wrinkled countenances which reflect the many experiences of their lives. One is my dear Great-Grandmother Kersey. Her face was deeply creased from the many physical and emotional stresses which she knew throughout her long life, but the goodness in her life glowed like sunshine through those "time lines."

The other person whom I immediately think of is Mother Theresa. Her countenance was marked by the deep crevasses which were formed through the years as she toiled and lived sacrificially among those in India whom she served. But her witness was not confined to India. Her life and witness stands as a beacon of God's love and compassion to many throughout the world as well.

Look at your face. Wear your wrinkles graciously because some of them are reflections of the inner beauty that God has created in your heart when you have attempted to serve Him and others.

The Art of Being Yourself

The German philosopher Authur Schopenhauer observed that "we forfeit three fourths of ourselves in order to be like other people." How tragic!

Because of recent scientific and technological breakthroughs, cloning makes front-page news. Scientists are now able to clone almost everything, and some want to try cloning human beings. President George W. Bush has strongly denounced the effort to do so.

God in His creative process has created each of us in His own image, yet each of us is a unique person. We are God-designed, one of a kind! As God's children we each occupy a special place in His great plan. No one is exactly like you or like me. After creating you and me, God threw away the molds. God forbid the day that we attempt to attain godhood and endeavor to clone another human. An unknown poet has written:

> That looking glass upon the wall
> Shows how you look, but that's not all.
> It says that you and only you,
> Can think your thoughts,
> Can have your fun,
> For you are you
> The only one.

Each of us is a genetic hybrid. We are a mixture of genes from a host of our ancestors. Recently my husband and I had a conversation about our genetic make up, our characteristics, and even our idiosyncrasies. Believe me, we all have them! I recognized that some of my qualities went back as far as my great-grandparents and the grandparents I had known, as well as my parents. From a deep concern about others and a strong desire to serve them, to my appreciation for all things of beauty (especially music), to a strong work ethic, to my enjoyment of being with people—these were all among my family characteristics.

A humorous prayer request by a Roman Catholic nun goes like this: "Dear Lord, help me to always accept the truth about myself, no matter how beautiful it may be!"

There are both major and minor chords in our lives. A favorite poet, Elizabeth Barrett Browning, said it this way: "With stammering lips and insufficient sounds, I strive and struggle to deliver right the music of my nature."

In our culture, we are often being pushed to be like someone else. Judy Garland once said, "Always be the first rate version of yourself rather than a second rate version of somebody else."

We must constantly remind ourselves that even that first rate version is not perfect. We are often too hard on ourselves when we forget that. Amish quilters intentionally put one mismatched piece in each quilt to remind themselves that they and their work cannot be perfect. Only God creates perfectly.

So, let us be who we are, and let us strive to be the best that we can be.

Just Being Is Enough

$\mathcal{I}$ grew up in a family where a very strong work ethic was practiced every day. I learned to work early in life, and I still like doing it. One of my special satisfactions has always been found in tallying the number of tasks I accomplish each day. This kind of pressure on myself has brought feelings of frustration—and even guilt—when my production level has dropped for even a short period of time. These feelings are disruptive elements in our life.

Pain has been my daily companion during much of my lifetime. During the past six months it has visited me with a renewed vengeance. A cycle of inactivity with a sense of frustration has also accompanied the pain. During this time, much of my reading and my conversations with two wise counseling friends have helped me to re-think the way I live each day. I am trying to learn to lean back, relax, and laugh. Having one good laugh before breakfast can set the tone for the day. We each need frequent flashes of fun, fun, fun! I am slowly learning to do this without having a blanket of guilt wrapped tightly around me. On my list of things to do today all I need to write are these words: breathe in, breathe out, breathe in, breathe out. . . .

These counselors have helped me realize when life's circumstances slow us down, we need to develop the art of just being. Being who I am is enough! We have long mistaken activity for achievement. Busy-ness does not equal productivity. Perhaps people are no longer human beings. Rather, we should be called human doings. Each person is rich because of who he is, rather than what he does or has.

Someone has suggested that being present to each day is enough. I realize I was here all day and that this is really all I need to do in a day. When evening comes, I can forget my list of "things to do" and how many projects I have checked off today. I was here all day. It has been so hard for me to realize that is what is really important. I was present to this day—present to this life, present to those around me, and I was even present to myself. My days are not counted by what I do, but what I am and that I was here all day. Reading the Psalms and quietly listening for God's voice have hastened the healing process for me. In Psalm 46:10a we are instructed to "Be still and know that I am God."

In his excellent book *The Finishing Touch*, Charles Swindoll comments on our persistent busy-ness and harried pace of living. He suggests: "If God is going to get our attention He better plan on (1) making an appointment with us, (2) taking a number, and (3) driving at least fifty-five miles per hour!" We must slow down and we must be quiet, if we would hear God's whispers to us.

I have just read another delightful book, *Dear Old Man* by Charles Wells. Dr. Wells was a noted geriatric psychiatrist and an admitted workaholic who wrote a series of letters to himself. He composed them during his active working years to be read and pondered later upon his retirement. One of his quotes which has captured my continued thinking is: "Making time in your life for doing nothing!" His thoughts are also helping me to practice another excellent suggestion to: "Take a little time each day to do whatever makes a happier you!" Yes, I must be reminded to make time for myself.

Another challenging book has been most helpful. In *Don't Sweat the Small Stuff—and It's All Small Stuff*, Dr. Richard Carlson gently offers this wise counsel: "Think of your problems as potential teachers."

Ah, yes, I must learn to have more patience with my physical limitations. I must use this slowing down time to develop more compassion for the hurts of others. I need to be more attentive to my Lord's guidance. Perhaps He is telling me to slow down, take a deep breath, and smell the roses which are literally blooming at our back door.

In Lewis Carroll's *Through the Looking Glass*, we are introduced to a delightful character called the Mad Hatter. He continually mixes his words and phrases in ways which present unusual meanings. A choice example is his admonition to Alice, "Don't just do something. Stand there!"

Just standing there is enough. Thank you, Lord, that just being is enough.

You Have the Choice

G od has never created a robot! God has created each of us with a free will to make choices. The choices we make will determine how we live our lives.

Every morning upon awakening we make a choice as to how we will meet and greet the day. We may choose to dwell on all the negatives in our life—the disappointments, the anxieties, the physical pain, the fear of the future. Or we may choose to focus on the positives in our life—a safe place, meaningful work, opportunities to serve others, the love of family and friends around us, and all forms of beauty God has given us.

In *Challenging Words*, Charles Swindoll writes:

> The longer I live, the more I realize the impact of attitude on life. The only thing we can play on is the one setting we have, and that is our attitude. . . . I am convinced that life is 10% what happens to me and 90% how I react to it. And so it is with you. . . . We are in charge of our attitudes!

Let our morning praise each day be: "This is the day the Lord has made. I will rejoice and be glad in it!"

We begin making choices very early in life and continue making them throughout our entire life journey. At a very young age babies make choices about the foods they find tasty. They are quick to turn their heads away from the spoonfuls of food they do not like. Young children want to choose the clothes they like and find comfortable to wear to school each day. Teenagers make important choices about their clothes, their friends, their habits of behavior, the moral standards they will live by, and the quality of their faith. Young adults make crucial choices when they decide on their career, their marriage partner, and faith-growing experiences.

Adults continually make choices regarding their attitudes toward those whom their lives touch, service to others, and decisions which affect the development of their faith. Older adults have to decide where they will live upon retirement, how they will invest their time, and how they can be of service to others.

There are basically two major kinds of choices that affect our lives: the choices we make over which we have control and the choices others make over which we have no control. They both affect us. For example, we may choose not to drink and drive our car in order to be as alert as possible, but someone else may choose to drink and drive his or her car and may crash into us, causing us bodily harm. That person exercises his or her right of choice over which we have no control, but our life is affected by that choice.

Paul Tournier reminded us: "Perhaps the most powerful and unused gift from God is the gift of choice."

Our lifetime consists of a series of choices. Some choices are very easy to make, others are very difficult. Of one thing we can be certain: God's gift of the freedom to choose will chart the course of our life.

To every man there opens a way, and ways, and a way—
And the high soul takes the high way,
And the low soul gropes the low.
And in between on the misty flats, the rest drift to and fro.
But to every man there openeth a high way and a low—
And every man decideth which way his soul shall go.
—John Oxenham

Thank you, God, for the choices we can make for ourselves. Please guide us as we make them. Amen.

Give Yourself Away

An ancient fable tells the story of two pools of mountain spring water. The two pools of sparkling clear water were nestled in two rocky pockets on the side of a mountain high above the plain below. They had come from the melting snow. One day as they were looking across the forests and plain that stretched out before them as far as they could see, the first pool said to the second pool, "I'm going to dash myself down the side of the mountain and into that rushing stream. I want to follow it way out beyond the blue horizon. Won't you come along with me?"

The second pool drew back from the rim of his rocky pocket and said, "No, thanks. I'm going to stay up here on the side of the mountain where it is nice and cool and where the mountain breezes blow. Besides, I don't know where that stream would take us and I'm sure I'd get all dirty. You go ahead. I'll stay here and wait for you."

The first pool bid his friend good-bye and, raising himself up, threw himself over the rim of his rocky pocket and found his way into the mountain stream that carried him rapidly down the side of the mountain. He noticed that the wild animals of the forest quenched their thirst with water from the stream. Some of the water was diverted into irrigation ditches and the crops took on new life as the water flooded over the fields. The farmers were pleased by the prospect of another bumper crop. The remaining water from the pool continued on through the irrigation ditches, then into a drainage ditch, into another stream, and eventually into the river which carried him into the sea. In the subsequent months the sun drew the water up from the sea, purified it, and dropped it down on the mountain again in the form of an autumn rain.

The pool wended his way down the side of the mountain until he was nestled in the same rocky pocket he had left in the spring. He could not wait to tell the second pool about his adventures. He began by saying, "That was the most wonderful experience that I have ever had. Every place I went I brought new life and hope. The animals quenched their thirst, the crops were revived, the farmers were happy. It was such a wonderful experience that I'm going to do it again. Won't you come along with me this time?" But there was no response from the second pool.

The first pool repeated his comments a bit louder. But still there was no response. Then the first pool raised himself up to look over the ridge that separated them in order to see the rocky pocket where the second pool had been resting. He was aghast! What had been a sparkling pool of clear mountain water was now just a stagnant pool whose very stench filled the air. In his attempt to save himself, he had lost his life; while the first pool had given his life away and had saved it.

Jesus said, "If you insist on saving your life, you will lose it. Only those who throw away their lives for my sake and for the sake of the Good News will ever know what it means to really live" (Matt. 8:35 THE LIVING BIBLE).

And so it is with you and me.

Oh, To Have a Faithful Friend

J am a "people" person. One of my special life needs is my need for friends. Life is empty and barren without meaningful relationships. From the time young children have their special playmates and throughout the mature years, there is joy—real joy—in sharing life's varied experiences with a friend.

- When there is a special joy in our life, that joy is doubled when we share it with a faithful friend.
- When great pressure is brought to bear on us at times, the comfort of a faithful friend will soften our strain and stress.
- When decisions of importance need to be made, the calm wisdom of a faithful friend helps us look more objectively at our different options.
- When difficult and tough times come to us, and they will, the love and support of a faithful friend will cut our sorrow and sadness in half.
- When we need wise counsel, a faithful friend will be completely honest and straightforward with us.
- When we fail to live at our best, a faithful friend will challenge us and will help us rise to a higher level.
- When others walk out of our life, a faithful friend walks in.
- When we are lonely and discouraged, a faithful friend wipes away our tears and helps us laugh again.

All of the above can be summarized in the quotation by B. DeAngelis who wrote: "Friends are angels who lift us to our feet when our own wings have trouble remembering how to fly."

A paraphrase from Ecclesiastes affirms that "a faithful friend is a source of shelter. Whoever has found one has found a rare treasure." When we become true friends in faith, the bonds of that rare treasure become impenetrable.

Don't be afraid to be a caring friend. You, too, may need one.

Softly It Falls

*U*pon awakening this morning, I lifted the shades on our bedroom windows. What a beautiful sight greeted me! On this February morning our first snow of the season was floating straight downward. The large lacey white flakes did not appear to be in a hurry to reach their destination. The rooftops on the houses across the street were already covered with soft downy blankets of pure white.

As I stood there enjoying this moment of God's beautiful handiwork, the words I had learned many years ago played across my mind, "Wash me, and I shall be whiter than snow" (Ps. 51:7 NRSV).

I can think of no other part of the natural world that brings us a sight as delicately gentle as softly falling snow. Often when we try to describe the snow we use two words: pure and white. As I sit and watch in fascination as the snow comes down, I realize that several things will happen to the snowflakes when they reach the earth.

Each snowflake as it falls is intricate, uniquely shaped, one of a kind, and like no other snowflake. However, it soon loses its identity as it touches and blends in with other snowflakes. Together they make up the beautiful blanket of snow which covers the ground. Before long they lose their purity and whiteness as we walk on them and drive over them. They are soon ground up into ugly gray slush. Each snowflake has been changed into something that is less than it was.

On this dark snowy morning, my mind continues to move on in its musings. I ask myself, "What is the value of this snow? What good does the snow ever do?" As I raise these questions, my eyes move to the pair of almost perfectly shaped blue spruce trees in our yard, and then I look over to the two majestic magnolias across the yard.

As I continue watching, I notice that the clouds are beginning to break up, the temperature is beginning to rise, and the newly fallen snow is beginning to thaw. As it turns to water, I realize that this additional moisture will help revive and sustain these trees and our lawn which suffered during the late summer and early fall months when our rainfall was inadequate. So, this snowfall suggests to me that this cycle of the natural order is but another one of the ways that God has designed to take care of the earth He has created.

The softly falling snow also reminds me that, like each snowflake, He has created you and me as unique persons. He has made only one of us. He has given each of us special gifts to use in ways that enrich our lives and the lives of others.

Dear Father, we thank you for the beauty of this freshly fallen snow, so white, so pure. Please wash me and I shall be whiter than snow. Amen.

Make the Commonplace Sacred

S hortly after my first book entitled *Queen Anne's Lace and Other Weeds* was released, I had an opportunity to try to make the commonplace sacred. Two delightfully charming sisters who host a very popular Saturday morning radio talk show had invited me to appear on their show. They had scheduled this show as a live remote broadcast from our local Barnes and Noble Bookstore. The show would have a live audience and special food would be served.

They had read a copy of my book and had called the person who was in charge of marketing at Providence House Publishers. They asked if I would be available for an interview. They had also chosen several meditations they wanted me to read and said they wanted me to remain after the broadcast to sign copies of the book.

When the publishing house relayed the request, I hesitated at first. They had already filled my summer schedule with a number of book signings. Then, after thinking about it a bit, I replied, "I'll be glad to do it. It will be another new experience for me." I had met a number of very interesting people in each of the previous signings.

When I arrived at the bookstore, Barbara, one of the sisters, handed me a copy of the schedule for the morning program. Then I began to wonder why I had said "yes" to the invitation. I was scheduled to be interviewed in the middle of several other interviews. The first interviewee was a representative from a well-known cigar company which specializes in Honduras tobacco cigars. The second interview was to be with a spokesperson from a local brewery which makes unusual kinds of beer. I was next. Following my interview, the chef from a popular new restaurant would talk about and give out samples of their fine food. The final interview would be the owner of a local dinner theater who wanted to put in a plug for the current play.

When the clock ticked away and it was my turn to take the microphone, I silently prayed, "God, help my words make this very commonplace a bit sacred today."

The hostesses were very casual and were excellent interviewers, and I thoroughly enjoyed the fourteen minutes with them. Also, I learned several new things that Saturday morning:

1. I learned there is a special etiquette to be followed in the way you light a cigar.
2. I learned some new words to add to my vocabulary. They included such terms as: lager, malt, and hops. But I have no idea how to use them.
3. I learned there is delicious food awaiting the diner at the restaurant when the chef served us a super herbal chicken pasta and a "to die for" Italian dessert. I never did learn how to pronounce the names of either one of them.
4. I learned about the plot of a comedy play which was new to me.

When the broadcast ended, the engineer handed me a copy of my book and quietly asked, "Would you please sign this for my daughter? There are some things in your book I want her to read."

It was then that I felt there may have been some sacred moments in that very commonplace corner of the bookstore that Saturday morning. I will never know.

Oh, What a Fragrance!

One year my husband gave me a gardenia plant as a Mother's Day gift. When he brought the plant home, it had several waxy white blossoms in full bloom. By the next morning, a wonderful fragrance had wafted throughout the house. The fragrance had even permeated our bedroom wing. What pleasant memories flooded my mind of high school proms and music recitals when I was given a gardenia corsage to wear.

Helen Keller said smells are potent wizards that transport us across thousands of miles and through all the years that we have lived. Judith Jackson, a certified aromatherapist, tells us that the sense of smell is one of our most powerful senses. It affects mind, body, and spirit. We are also told that the cells of our nasal passages send sharp signals to the area of the brain that triggers learning, emotions, and memory.

Down through the ages people have believed that there is a restorative and comforting power in fragrances which soothe our bodies and souls. There is archeological evidence that the Chinese people may have been the first to extract aromatic oils as early as three thousand years before Christ. In other great civilizations of the world, including Egypt and Rome, they mixed oils and extracts from fragrant flowers and herbs for medicinal purposes.

In 1928 a French chemist, Rene' Maurice Gattefosse, coined the word "aromatherapy" when he concluded that the nose and skin help convey therapeutic benefits from aromatic oils to other parts of the body.

Fragrances have long been associated with special moments in my garden of memories. I remember:

- the pungent fragrance of newly mown alfalfa hay on a hot Iowa summer night which brings happy memories of my "growing up" years;
- the fragrance of cold cream which brings my Grandmother Martin's sweet face before me because she always used it at bedtime;
- the fragrance of baby powder which enfolds me with memories of my precious daughter's baby days;
- the fragrance of the mock orange which reminds me of the bush which bloomed beside Grandmother Crosley's house and those special talks we had while sitting in her porch swing on hot summer evenings;
- the fragrance of my husband's tangy aftershave which helps me recall the strength of his shoulder when I grieved over the loss of my father.

For me, fragrances and memories are always tied together with ribbons of love.

The apostle Paul spoke of an ultimate fragrance when he wrote: "But thanks be to God, who . . . through us spreads everywhere the fragrance of the knowledge of Him. For we are the aroma of Christ among those who are being saved" (2 Cor. 2:14–15 NIV).

Paul believed that when Christ is the center of our lives, we exude the fragrance of His presence. This thought brings one of my favorite prayers of Mother Theresa to mind: "Help me spread the fragrance of Jesus wherever I go." Amen!

Old and Everlasting

We love New England, especially in the autumn during the brilliant foliage season. We also enjoy "antiquing." When you combine the two, you have the makings of a delightful trip to this special corner in God's world.

One year our itinerary took us to a unique shop in an old weathered barn on a quiet country road in the Finger Lake region of New York state. A carpet of green lined with colorful vats of flowers marked the path from our car to the front door of the barn. "Old and Everlasting" was the name the shopkeeper had given to her barn of goodies. As we looked at the old barn it was evident that it had weathered many blustery New England winters with heavy snows as well as drenching summer rains. It had survived them all!

"Old and Everlasting" causes me to think of faithfulness, integrity, honesty, respect, dependability, responsibility, trustworthiness, and love. Ah! These are surely the qualities of life by which to live.

Today we are hearing the rustle of many refreshing winds of social and spiritual change. One of the most exciting I have heard of during the last few years is the Promise Keeper movement. This movement was born in the heart and mind of Bill McCartney, the former coach of the University of Colorado national championship football team.

Promise Keepers is designed to challenge men to a life committed to Jesus Christ as their Savior and Lord and to pledge themselves to be responsible and caring husbands and fathers. Surely this is one expression of values which is old and everlasting.

A nationally syndicated columnist has observed: "Something is stirring in the land. It's too early to call it a third Great Awakening like those preceding the American Revolution and the Civil War." But he pointed out that many believe that Promise Keepers has emerged as another very significant answer to the pervasive deep spiritual hunger in our society that has become evident in so many ways. Many of us watched on our television screens as thousands of men stood shoulder-to-shoulder on the Washington, D.C., mall. They formed a literal carpet of men. Many of them stood for six hours as they prayed, sang, and pledged themselves to renewed levels of commitment to lives of service, love, and faithful living.

Soon after that unusual display of faith and commitment, a letter to the editor appeared in our local newspaper. It had been written by a young woman who was twenty years old. She said she hoped she might someday be married to a Promise Keeper kind of man—one who would love Jesus Christ first and his wife a close second!

The bountiful abundance of life which Christ promised to His followers comes when we claim the old, the solid, the enduring values and relationships and blend them with our dreams for the future. Only then will we be equipped to help make this world which God has loaned to us an even better one of everlasting hope.

Signs Along the Highway

"Life is God's gift to you,
What you do with it is your gift to God."

Those words, in large bold letters, were on the back of a large semi-trailer that we were following on an interstate highway. I felt good when I read the sign, and assumed that the driver just ahead of us was probably a Christian.

The words on the back of that truck continued to echo in my mind as we drove along the highway. I realized that as Christians, we do owe everything to God as we travel down life's highway. I recall reading an insight that went something like this:

Your life and everything around you are simply on loan for you to use while you are here. Please take good care of yourself as my child. Take good care of the earth around you. Share what I have given you with others around you who are also my children. This total package will be your gift back to me.

The word we hear most often to describe this relationship with God and the world around us is stewardship. Stewardship is an attitude of life about who we are, where we live, and what we have.

God has created us in His image. The apostle Paul went as far as to say our bodies are where God lives in us while we are on earth. Read his words:

> Do you not know that your body is a temple of the Holy Spirit within you, which you have from God, and that you are not your own? For you were bought with a price; therefore, glorify your body (1 Cor. 6:19–20 NRSV).

Paul believed that God expects us to take care of the place where He lives in us. To me, this means I should try to maintain a healthy lifestyle, should fill my mind with good thoughts, and should practice spiritual disciplines to nourish my soul.

God expects us to take care of the earth that He has loaned to us. Not long ago as we drove behind a sports utility vehicle, we noticed that the driver was tossing things out the open window—a napkin, a sandwich container, and a candy bar wrapper. As we passed the car, I saw that the lone occupant was a young driver. Either his parents had not taught him by example how to care for God's world, or he had completely forgotten the lesson.

In her little book, *In My Own Words*, Mother Teresa wrote:

> Whoever is dependent only on his or her money, or even worries about it is truly a poor person. But, if that person places his or her money at the service of others, then that person becomes rich, very rich indeed.

Mother Teresa was the living embodiment of giving God's gift of life back to Him. She completely gave her mind, her minutes, and the money that was given to her by others.

Many of us wear colored glasses with dollar signs on the lens. They keep us blinded to all the needs around us. Our love of things will always betray us and will cause us to forget the true values in life.

> Dear Father, may we always remember to be grateful that you have given us life in the right place at the right time. Help us guard against being selfish with it. Help us practice the disciplines that will nurture our souls, our earth, and those around us. Amen.

Living on the Edge

At a dinner party, we were reminiscing with our guests about a mutual friend who is a seminary professor. One man said what he remembered most about the professor was his insistence that "you are never doing your best work unless you are on the edge of your incompetence."

I subscribe to this credo for my life. We are seldom doing our best unless we are living at the very edge of our own incompetence. I believe we should always strive to do and be better, better, better. . . .

- Every time I put together a floral design, I want it to be more creative than the last one I did.
- Every time I prepare and serve a dinner menu I want it to be tastier than the last time I prepared and served that menu.
- Every time I polish an antique copper kettle I want it to be shinier and have more patina than the last time I cleaned it.
- Every time I speak with a hurting friend, I want to be more understanding and helpful than the last time I called her.
- Every time I write a meditation, I want it to be more helpful and healing than the last one I wrote.

As believers in Christ, we know that without Christ in our lives we continue to live in the comfort of our own incompetence, our own inadequacy, and our own insufficiency. When He is absent from our lives, we are not the effective vessels we could be if He were fully present in our lives.

What is more, when Christ is not the dominating force in our lives, there are pockets of self-centeredness which tend to crowd out those things which make up the abundant life that He offers. We must learn how to empty ourselves. We must learn how to move over and let Him take over. The apostle Paul struggled with this and when writing to the church in Philippi, he wrote: "Not that I have already obtained this or have reached the goal; but I press on to make it my own, because Christ Jesus has made me his own . . . this one thing I do: forgetting what lies behind and straining forward to what lies ahead, I press on toward the goal for the prize of the heavenly call of God in Christ Jesus" (Phil. 3:12–14 NRSV).

Only as we, too, strain to live beyond our own self-centered incompetence can we find fulfillment in Him. Then, we can affirm with the apostle Paul, "I can do all things through Him who strengthens me" (Phil. 4:13 NRSV).

The Art of Homecaring

The homemaking classes I took as an eighth grader and as a high school student in the Iowa school system were some of my favorite courses during all of my years of schooling. The lessons I learned at school were strongly reenforced by my mother at home. Many of us grew up in a generation when learning to care for a home was a sacred art. I learned how to bake a loaf of bread, how to sort the white clothes from the colored ones on wash day, and how to iron a shirt. (My father would lovingly comment that he always knew when Mary had ironed his shirts—much to my mother's delight.) I learned how to set a dinner table correctly, how to fold a napkin properly as it was ironed, and how to whip an angel food cake by hand in a large heavy crock bowl with an antique wire wisp. (The crock and the wire wisp were part of my dowry when I married.)

The creative part of me responded to each learning experience when my teacher or my mother taught me something new. Creating and maintaining an orderly and attractive home still gives me great satisfaction. I get a lift from cleaning out a cupboard, polishing an antique copper kettle, or arranging the roses my husband brings in from his garden.

During the 1960s the book *The Feminine Mystique* became a bible for many women and helped influence them to leave their homes in droves for the workplace. Betty Friedan, the author, assured women that they would find complete fulfillment in the marketplace outside their homes. For some women it was (and still is) financially necessary to work outside their homes, but for others that is not the case. Many have discovered during these past three decades that there is much tedium and monotony in many of these paying jobs and they feel "run ragged." Furthermore, society is now reaping an unbelievable amount of child and youth delinquency. Recent research has shown the critical importance of having adequate parental guidance in the home.

Sarah Ban Breathnach, in her refreshing book *Simple Abundance*, suggests we need to recover the "sacred soulcraft of homecaring." She writes, "Creating a beautiful, orderly, well-run home can be among our most satisfying accomplishments as well as an illuminating spiritual experience. Channeling your time and creative energy closer to home will produce a big emotional return for you and for those you love."

Having come full circle in my life as a music teacher for many years and as a national workshop leader to a full-time home caregiver, I know I find less physical stress and greater emotional and spiritual returns in my home than in any other place.

Gunilla Norris wrote, "My life will always have dirty dishes. If this sink can become a place of contemplation, let me learn constancy here."

Brother Lawrence was a very special monk of the Middle Ages whose responsibility in the monastery where he was cloistered was working in the kitchen. He felt this to be his sacred calling. His well-known poem, "Lord of All Pots and Pans," has become synonymous with the sacred in the commonplace. I have always admired the simple and serene lives of the Amish and Quaker women whose lives center around their homes and families.

Our homes are a reflection of our personality, of who we really are. At times when I observe the lives and activities of some of those around me, it seems they "keep on the go" to avoid being at home with themselves. For many, homecaring has become an endangered calling. It often takes more patience and creativity to take care of the trivial—but very necessary—tasks of everyday living in the home than to work in the more visible and monumental positions of the business and professional world outside the home.

During the month of May we celebrate Mother's Day, and we are made more aware of the importance of the Christian home and our place in it; I am so thankful for my home. Here I may become renewed through the challenges to my own creativity and the support of my loved ones. Surely, our homes are places to be protected and cherished.

From the wisdom found in the Book of Proverbs comes this affirmation: "She watches carefully all that goes on in her household and is never lazy. Her children stand and bless her; so does her husband. He praises her with these words: 'There are many fine women in the world, but you are the best of them all'" (31:27–29 OLB).

He Listens and He Answers

He Listens and He Answers

F have lived long enough to thank God that all my prayers have not been answered in the way I prayed they would be. When it seems God does not respond to our cries for help and does not grant our prayer requests, many times we feel God is not listening. But, He is constantly listening with a heart full of love and caring. He wants only the highest and the best for us now and for eternity.

> If radio's slim fingers can pluck a melody from night . . . and toss
>   it over continent or sea;
> If the petaled white notes of a violin are blown across the moun-
>   tains or the city's din;
> If songs, like crimson roses, are culled from thin blue air,
> Why should mortals wonder if God hears prayer?
> —Ethel Romig Fuller

Often our prayers as we pray them are not granted, but God does answer each petition in ways that are ultimately best for us and for others around us. Our God is a God of order and constancy as well as a God of love. He has created the universe with certain natural and physical laws which operate within and throughout all forms of the natural order, including the world about us as well as our own bodies.

When we or others ignore some of the natural laws, catastrophes such as fires and floods may result. When we or others ignore some of the physical laws that operate in our bodies, illness and disease may result.

Sometimes the intricate web of parts in our bodies become entangled or go awry through no fault of our own. At other times things go awry because we or others make unwise decisions or choices. When those conditions occur in our bodies we experience brokenness. God's laws do not change, nor does He abandon us or stop loving us.

Some years ago, our daughter lost an eye. She was sixteen years old at the time. Many in our neighborhood, in our church, and in our seminary prayed that her eyesight might be saved. Those prayers were not granted, but God did answer in a different manner and used the situation to help others grow in their faith. Many, including an agnostic physician in the operating room, were touched by the strength of her faith in Jesus Christ. A young seminary student was uncertain about his call to the ministry. After learning of her faith and continued confidence in God, he told one of his professors that her witness convinced him that God was calling him into His service as a minister.

The apostle Paul prayed over and over again that his handicap, which he called his "thorn in the flesh," might be removed. God did not grant Paul the answer he sought, but He did answer the prayer by giving him the grace and strength to live with it triumphantly.

Dwight L. Moody, the great evangelist of the last century, encouraged his hearers to "Spread out your petitions before God, and then say, 'Thy will be done.' The sweetest lesson I have learned in God's school is to let the Lord choose for me!"

> Slowly, oh, so slowly I have learned
> To wait the answer coming soon or late.
> So often in the past I prayed then turned
> Refusing in my eagerness to wait,
> Yet, even so the good God,
> Who had heard, answered every word.
> Surely, I shall wait patiently today,
> Knowing the answered prayer is on its way.
>
> —Author Unknown

God always brings some positive things out of the negative experiences in our lives if we are but patient and trust Him. Our traumas can be turned to triumphs in God's gracious hands. Our dark nights will be turned into bright mornings. For as the Lord told Isaiah: "As the heavens are higher than the earth, So my ways are higher than your ways and my thoughts than your thoughts" (Isa. 55:9 NIV).

We Need Each Other

A familiar roadside picture in many parts of rural America shows:

> Rusting roofs on sagging barns near
> Abandoned windowless houses that are
> Wrapped in tall grasses and weeds growing in
> Unkempt and long neglected yards. . . .

They are graphic reminders of the sweeping economic changes brought on by World War II in the forties which caused many families to leave their old homesteads and move to other places throughout the states in unprecedented numbers. Additional cultural changes in the late twentieth century have further undercut the family, small towns, and rural supports many of us have known.

I grew up in a small town in the rich farmlands of central Iowa. My father had a business on Main Street that was related to those who lived on the land. Everyone knew everyone else as they went about their activities of the day on Main Street and throughout the village. Within two short blocks there were four churches of four different denominations located on four corners.

There was a strong sense of community there. My mother figuratively and humorously described the community as a place where everyone knew when she threw her dishwater out the back door. (Although we did have modern plumbing.) Or, as another person expressed it: "The nice thing about living in a small town is that when we aren't sure what we are doing, someone else always knows."

I am grateful that I grew up in that small community of "grassroots" people. They had a deep sense of commitment to the land, to their families, and to God. That is truly a rich heritage, indeed!

Today's sense of community, however, is not limited to a time in history or to a small dot on a map. A community is a spirit, an attitude, that is built on relationships among loving and caring persons. Regardless of where we live, we are part of some kind of neighborhood:

- in a small crossroads village,
- in a cluster of farm homes,
- in a retirement community,
- in a county seat town,
- in a health care facility,
- in a suburban development, or
- in a downtown urban area.

Every neighborhood can have a sense of community. Some may be saying, "But that is not true anymore." Granted, it is much harder today to create a sense of community than it was even fifty years ago. It takes a bit of doing on the part of everyone. There are many little things we can do to show we care:

- sharing a bouquet of homegrown roses with one who is ill,
- taking a loaf of freshly baked bread or a plate of cookies to a new neighbor as the moving van pulls into the driveway,
- pushing a health care center resident down the hall in her wheel chair,
- phoning a friend to ask about her daughter who has just had surgery, or
- reading to a friend who can no longer see well enough to read.

I now live in a suburban neighborhood where there is a real sense of community. There are many differences among us: in our occupations, our ages, our ethnic heritages, our geographic backgrounds, our denominational affiliations, and the size of our families. However, these differences are all laid aside as we share in each others' lives through the joys and sorrows that come to each of us. Recently, we said our final good-byes to a very dear friend in our neighborhood who succumbed to a fatal illness and, during that same week, we celebrated the safe arrival of triplets whose grandparents live across the street.

Finally, I have concluded that our lives are not completely fulfilled until we are a part of God's own divine community which we know as His Church. It is here in the church community that Christ bids us to love God with our hearts, our souls, and our minds, and to love our neighbors as ourselves!

The Great Catcher

$\mathscr{A}$lmost everyone I know loves the circus. I grew up in the era when the great circuses traveled from city to city. Our little town was much too small to attract one of those traveling wonders, so my grandfather took me at a very young age to see the famous Ringling Brothers circus which was performing in a larger town nearby. It was the thrill of my young lifetime!

This trip with my grandfather held a double excitement for me. It came as a celebration trip following major orthopedic surgey and many long months of therapy as I learned to walk again. The anticipation and joy of that day is still safely locked in the bank of my happy childhood memories.

Some years ago we took our two grandchildren, Amy and Hart, to see their first circus. We went to Peru, Indiana, to visit special friends and to see the unique amateur circus which is offered there every summer. Peru is full of circus memories. The International Circus Hall of Fame is located there, and for over one hundred years Peru has laid claim to the title of "The Circus Capital of the World." Large barns at the edge of Peru served for a number of years as the winter quarters for the animals of one of our nation's major circuses.

During the last thirty years literally hundreds of children and youth have been trained to perform in Peru's amateur circus in their own permanent "big top" arena. Recently, eight of those teenagers, ages thirteen to eighteen years, who call themselves the Young Americans, were inducted into the *Guiness Book of World Records* for successfully performing the first eight-person pyramid on the high wire. As a result of this feat, they were invited to compete in the 1999 International Amatuer Circus Meet in Monte Carlo.

There were no animals in the circus we watched with our grandchildren because all the performers were children and youth from the area. We sat amazed as we witnessed their agility, strength, and skills as they balanced on the high wires, juggled flame daggers, performed bungee aerobics, and soared through the air on the flying trapeze. As we watched these young flyers and their catchers perform amazing feats in mid-air, several thoughts came to mind:

1. These young people had developed a high level of trust in themselves. This confidence was obviously achieved through the long months of disciplined training in which each had been involved.
2. They had developed a deep sense of trust in each other, whether balancing in that eight-person pyramid on the high wire or flying high on the trapeze into the hands of their catcher.
3. Perhaps the trapeze act showed the greatest level of trust as they flew across that abyss of empty space into the grasp of their catcher—that catcher whose timing was so crucial, for he had to be in just the right spot at exactly the right time. The catcher made the difference between success or failure, safety or catastrophe.

By nature I have never been a risk taker. Perhaps a fear of embarrassment, disappointment, or even failure has held me back. But if we are to live life to its fullest, we must take some risks. As we learn to become risk takers, we realize that it is very necessary to develop an attitude of trust. A deep level of trust must always be our silent partner to accompany and guide us as we learn to fly beyond the boundaries of our levels of comfort. Without trust we live our lives fearfully, anxiously, unsurely, and insecurely.

Life's experiences have taught me that we must sometimes take risks at every age if we hope to offer some small shining gift to those around us. Our finest dreams become real in those moments when we become willing to try a new thing—willing to risk. They can become life-size. They will take shape 1) as we trust in ourselves, through our own faithful discipline;

2) as we love and trust those who help us along the way; and most importantly, 3) as we learn to trust God more completely day by day.

We will never feel the security of His strong arms catching us, holding us, and lifting us unless we stretch our arms across the chasms of risk and uncertainty toward Him in trust, believing He is our Great Catcher. The writer of Deuteronomy reminds us that "The eternal God is our refuge, and underneath are His everlasting arms" (33:27 NIV). What better way to move out in this New Year than to be caught and held by the Great Catcher?

A Little Touch, A Big Miracle

I am a person who needs to give and receive lots of touches and hugs. In many countries and cultures around the world such open demonstrations of affection are not practiced nor are they even considered to be acceptable behavior. However, God has created in all living creatures the innate need to be touched.

A premature baby is repeatedly touched by the neonatal nurses who care for it. Parents of this wee one don hospital gowns to rock and caress their new child as they bond with him or her while the baby is still in the hospital.

Researchers tell us that abandoned and neglected children placed in isolated orphanages in other parts of the world are oftimes stunted in their physical and social growth because their limited caregivers have not had the time to give them many loving touches. These children have difficulty accepting love later due to the long periods of isolation in cribs by themselves.

A cross-cultural comparison of the playground behavior exhibited by preschoolers in France and in the United States yields some very interesting data. The children in France touched each other twice as much when playing with one another as did the American children. Also, the French children acted aggressively toward one another only 1 percent of the time, while their American counterparts acted aggressively 29 percent of the time.

Other studies show that France has the lowest homicide rate among all developed countries, while the United States has the highest rate. The late

Margaret Mead, world reknown anthropologist, found in her study of the New Guinea people that when children were showered with affection during their early years, there were fewer incidences of violent behavior among them when they became adults. Such findings indicate that there is a direct link between the amount and quality of touching experienced by small children and the amount of violent behavior they exhibit as adults.

I was fortunate to grow up in an openly affectionate family, and it is a tradition that is still continued today. When my college-age grandson, Hart, bounds in the door, gives me a warm hug, and greets me with, "I love you, Granny!" it turns on a bright light for me.

Our granddaughter, Amy, began her teaching career by working with early elementary high-risk children. She soon became aware of their need for many loving touches alongside much positive discipline in order that they might learn non-violent ways of relating to one another.

We recall that much of the ministry of Jesus was marked by the different ways He touched others: He held little children; He washed the feet of His disciples; He touched the eyes of the blind man; He touched the untouchable lepers; and the woman in need of healing reached out and touched the hem of His garment.

Where did we go wrong in our pseudo-sophisticated and often perverted society where any form of touch is so easily misused or misunderstood? What has happened to us that we are so reluctant to express our concern and care for one another with such a simple act as reaching out and touching one another?

I may be old fashioned but I believe that:

- a student still needs the pat of a teacher as commendation for work well done;
- a patient still needs the gentle touch of a doctor's hand given in encouragement;
- a lonely person still needs a hug from a friend;
- a parishioner still needs the hug or firm handclasp of a dedicated pastor in times of joy and in times of trauma.

We can never fully know the joys or hurts other persons carry in their hearts at any given moment. Our touch may bring healing or celebration for another pilgrim we meet on the pathway.

Each of us also needs the touch of Jesus in our soul. His healing touch has always brought the miracle of wholeness to body, mind, and spirit. The words of a Gaither hymn say it well:

> He touched me, O, He touched me, and O, the joy that floods my
> soul!
> One thing happened, so now I know, He touched me and made
> me whole.

Let us give thanks for human and heavenly touches.

From Darkness to Light

The mass media, through both the written and spoken word, regularly barrages us with negative accounts of world happenings and events. At the beginning of the new millennium, efforts were made to alert us to all of the catastrophic possibilities that could occur at the dawn of the new century. They warned us of computer "glitches" which could have caused us to lose our water supply, our electricity, our supplies of fuel, our money in our banking systems, and even our food supplies.

In the aftermath of the September 11 attacks, frequently asked questions have been, "Are you afraid?" and "How have you been affected by the attacks?" and "Do you think there are any terrorists hiding out in your community?" These and other similar questions tend to generate fear among us.

Fear has knocked on the door of my heart many times through the years, but most of my fearful feelings have been of my own making. Many of us fear change, separation from our loved ones through distance or death, health problems, a sense of loneliness, or the unknown.

We fear change for it takes away our established comfort zones. We fear separation from our loved ones through relocation, estrangement, or death because we all want to be close to our nearest and dearest. We fear health failure for it can bring pain and can often change our outlook on life. We fear loneliness for we are created as social beings and need the company of others. We fear the unknown—possibly most of all—because the uncertainty of what the future will bring is out of our control.

Fear is no stranger to anyone. Even the disciples who had lived in the presence of Jesus knew fear. They cowered in fear for their lives after Jesus was crucified and buried.

Fear is a powerful negative emotion. Fear can destroy. Fear can take away our strength and confidence. Fear can diminish our ability to think clearly and to act with confidence. And fear can paralyze our decision-making processes.

A large sign on the front window of a Christian Science reading room read, "Learn to live without fear." Yes, that is essential for us if we hope to fully experience the abundant life, but how do we achieve that? In a letter to young Timothy, the apostle Paul wrote: "For God has not given us the spirit of fear; but of power, and of love, and of a sound mind" (2 Tim. 1:7 KJV). Paul and untold numbers of Christians have discovered that faith in the goodness and steadfastness of God is surely the healing balm that enables us to live positively when we are confronted with those things which are fearful.

Faith in God enables us to see the changes that the future may bring not as problems but as opportunities. Through faith we can face the uncertainties of national and world events with a quiet confidence in Him who created us and sustains us. Through faith we can know that even in separation we will be joined with family here and in the future. Through faith our health problems can be faced with confidence in the skilled hands and minds of our physicians who are co-laborers with God. Through faith we realize that we can ease our loneliness by reaching out to help others in their life journey. Faith enables us to consider the unknown as a wonderful and exciting challenge.

> Fear knocked on the door. Faith opened it and there was no one there.
>
> —Author Unknown

> "Come to the Edge," life said.
> They said, "We are afraid."
> "Come to the Edge," life said.
> They came.
> It pushed them—and they flew!
>
> —Guillaume Apollinaire
> 1870–1918

Enrichment

One of the most beautiful stories of friendship ever told is recorded for us in the Bible. Jonathan, the prince of Judah, and a young shepherd boy named David had pledged their friendship in the name of the Lord. The Philistine giant, Goliath, had threatened Jonathan's father, King Saul, and had laid down a challenge to fight anyone whom the generals from Judah would name to represent them. David volunteered to fight Goliath and slew him with a stone from his slingshot. He was then highly acclaimed and given much praise as a national hero.

Saul became very envious of the handsome young David's popularity. Jealousy ate holes of hatred in King Saul's heart, and his passionate anger caused his mind to become warped. He devised a clever plot to kill David, but when Jonathan learned of his father's plot, he devised a counter-plan to save David's life—even though it meant turning away from his own father. It is a fascinating story of how strong the bond of true friendship can be. Jonathan loved David as he loved himself. I invite you to read the whole story. You will find it recorded in the Old Testament book of 1 Samuel in chapters 18, 19, and 20.

An old Scandinavian proverb declares "the finger of God touches you when you make a friend." Surely heaven comes down to touch us when we have faithful friends in our hearts. Here are some of the ways friendships have enriched my life:

There is always an uplifting joy in deep friendships. A friend sent these thoughts to me on the Internet: "Friends are like an upside-down rainbow.

Their smiles bring the sun and they fill the ho-hum moments with laughter and fun." A very dear friend of mine always takes the "ho-hum" out of almost every ordinary situation. She has a special knack for taking many very normal experiences and turning them into hilarious moments. When we get together we still find ourselves shaking with hysterical laughter as we recall some of the episodes we have experienced together through the years.

Special friends bring comfort and security when our hearts and minds are troubled or sad. As friends, we may receive comfort and give comfort at the same time. We each feel we have found a haven of safety and security when this happens.

Nancy Alleta Ayer passes on this upbeat suggestion: "Learn to greet your friends with a smile; they carry too many frowns in their own hearts to be bothered with yours." It was Ralph Waldo Emerson who observed that "Friendship, like the immortality of the soul, is too good to believe. When friendships are real, they are not glass threads or frostworks, but the solidest things we know." A friend is someone who can bring a warm touch of caring to any situation just by being there.

I have found that a friend senses the gifts that another person has to give and is able to pull those gifts out so they might be shared with others. Anaïs Nin must have been thinking along this line when she wrote: "Each friend represents a world in us, a world possibly unborn until they arrive, and it is only by this meeting that a new world of potential is born."

I have concluded that anything worthwhile in life is costly. Nurturing a friendship requres much commitment. An old admonition encourages us to "Go often to the house of thy friend, for weeds choke up the unused path." Such a continuing effort results in relationships that move beyond the ordinary. It was the Indian poet Tagore who captured this thought in these beautiful words, "After you had taken your leave, I found God's footprints on my floor."

Dear Father, we thank you for giving us wonderful friendships as part of your plan for our lives. And, most of all, we praise you for coming to us in Jesus Christ, our Divine Friend. Amen.

Please Wash Me, Lord

We were having one of those early spring rainstorms. There were flashes of lightning, jarring thunderclaps, and heavy pellets of rain beating rhythms against the bay window in our bedroom. As I prepared for bed I wondered if I could sleep. Soon the intruding noise settled down to the comforting sound of a gentle steady rain. I felt my body relax as I pulled the covers closer around me and deep sleep came swiftly.

Some hours later, bright beams of sunshine filtered through the window shades and beckoned me to the experiences of a new day. As I pulled up the shades, I saw the refreshed and dripping earth spread out before me. Sparkling puddles of water danced in the street. The dark green leaves on the holly bush outside my window were beautifully adorned with tiny droplets of rain. The leaves served as a lush background for the red berries which the birds had somehow overlooked during the winter months. Our favorite ever-present front yard sentinel, a restless mockingbird, was perched on our horse-head hitching post. That seemed to be his favorite lookout for keeping an eye on the territory he had staked out and claimed as his own. At a more distant bird feeder, our cardinals were breaking open their morning breakfast of sunflower seeds. They appeared to be refreshed and hungry after the long stormy night.

As I contemplated the scene before me, I sensed one of God's gentle nudges, "Write down a description of what you are seeing this morning."

My thoughts went back momentarily to my college days more than fifty years earlier to a poem which I had used as a devotional thought for a group. My mental computer had pulled up the title of the poem, "I Saw God Wash the World." After some time I located it in our library of favorite books. These inspiring thoughts were written by a well-known pastor of the early twentieth century.

I saw God wash the world last night
With His sweet shower on high;
And then when morning came
I saw Him hang it out to dry.

He washed each tiny blade of grass,
And every trembling tree;
And He flung His showers against the hills
And swept the billowy sea.

The white rose is a cleaner white;
The red rose is more red
Since God washed every fragrant face
And put them all to bed. . . .

I saw God wash the world last night;
Ah, would He had washed me
As clean of all my dust and dirt
As that old white birch tree!

—Dr. William L. Stidger

Dear Father, please wash me clean.

Clean out my pride of self, and
Fill me with humility of spirit.

Clean out my self-pity as I struggle, and
Fill me with gratitude for your strength.

Clean out my jealousy of others, and
Fill me with joy in their achievement.

Clean out my weakness to witness, and
Fill me with courage to share my convictions.

Clean out my disdain of others who are different, and
Fill me with love, even as You love all Your children.

Clean out my selfishness in ownership, and
Fill me with a generosity in all things.

Please wash me clean, O Lord!

The Home Front

*W*hen we celebrate Mother's Day, we also recognize the importance of the Christian home. The secular and religious traditions of different cultures of the past have attached varied degrees of importance to the role that women have played in the structures of their societies.

Thoughout the history of the Hebrew people as recorded in the Old Testament, there is an interesting cycle in the changing role of women. In the very beginning, woman was created by God to be a "help meet" (help mate) partner with man as his equal. The first three books of the law, Genesis, Exodus, and Leviticus, clearly indicated that a woman should be honored, feared, and obeyed. Motherhood was a sacred trust. The woman named the children in the family. She was responsible for their early education. A woman attended the religious gatherings for worship. She brought her own separate sacrifices and offered them up in worship. She was exempt from all labor on the Sabbath. And, if there were no male heirs, she could inherit and own property.

The relationship between a husband and wife at that time was compared to the sacred relationship which existed between Israel and Yahweh. Life in those days was very simple. It centered around the primary family and their nomadic lifestyle.

As the years passed their culture became more complicated. For example, by the period of the judges, the role of women had deteriorated severely. There was a growing tendency to look on women as being inferior to men. Some women were considered to be cheap chattel, some were even assigned roles as slaves. They could go only as far as the outer courtyard surrounding the Temple and were not allowed to go in the Temple with the men.

We remember the story of the Hebrew mother Naomi and her daughter-in-law, Ruth, who was a Gentile Moabite. When their husbands both died and they were widowed, they were considered to be social outcasts. They survived only because Boaz and other caring Hebrew landowners permitted them to gather up the leftover grain along the edges of the field. The lot of women was at a very low ebb.

Jesus Christ left His footprints throughout the pages of the New Testament; He changed that. Many women played very important roles in His life, beginning with His own mother, Mary. As was the custom for all Jewish mothers, she trained Him in those early tender years of His life. Surely, God was her teacher, for she was little more than a child herself when He was born. I can see her taking His small hand in hers as they walked through the streets of their village, Nazareth. Perhaps she let Him pet a little puppy or helped Him pick up pretty stones along the path.

I can imagine she cuddled Him in her lap and wiped his tears as she soothed his cuts and bruises which every boy experiences when playing outside. I'm certain she taught Him well in the tradition of their Hebrew faith. Perhaps there were special times when she even tried to prepare Him for the great mission which He was to undertake in the years to come.

There were other women who touched His life even as He changed theirs. I think of the Samaritan woman at the well; his friends Mary and Martha; Mary Magdeline; Mary, the mother of James and John; the woman who was caught in the act of adultery; and others.

Moving to another time and place, I am reminded of the pioneer women of our country. They were strong women in a simple culture where they worked shoulder-to-shoulder with their husbands. Together they carved out new homes and new lives for their families. They taught their children the simple lessons of hard work as they claimed the land. They helped them learn the difference between right and wrong, and they demonstrated a strong faith in God in this new land of freedom and opportunity.

As the years passed and as the satisfaction and security in a simple home-life gave way to our more sophisticated and complicated ways, the role of modern women has undergone drastic changes. Beginning in the 1960s women began to look outside their homes to "find themselves." Many felt they could be fulfilled only in the marketplace. For some women it was and still is an economic necessity. For others, they felt they must escape from the boredom of the daily routines in their homes.

For many children it meant that much of their teaching and training was relegated to caregivers in daycare centers and after-school programs. For others, it marked the emergence of a new generation of "latchkey" children. Is it possible that the changes in our new economy coupled with the all-too-common desire to own more and better "things" have jeopardized the quality of our home life?

Much of my recent reading and study informs me that many women are now leaving the job market with its "rat race." They are downsizing and simplifying their lifestyles in order to claim once again their role as keepers of the home. An increasing number of mothers are home-schooling their children. Unfortunately, our society has tried to remove simple moral and ethical teaching or anything hinting of religion from the public classroom. Therefore, many mothers are reclaiming their responsibility for the spiritual nurture and development of their children.

I continue to ask myself, "What is our role as Christian women in today's world?"

We, Too, Can Fly

*L*ast year we planted a butterfly bush alongside our deck. This year the bush has doubled in size and has produced twice as many long lavender blooms which adorn the graceful branches. I watched in fascination as a beautiful dark-colored swallowtail butterfly flitted over and around the blooms. He dipped down here and there deftly taking sweet nectar for nourishment.

I was reminded of the man who found a large cocoon. He placed the cocoon in a spot where he could observe it several times a day as he passed by. One day he noticed a small opening in the side of the cocoon. He was truly fascinated as he watched a newly-hatched butterfly as it pushed and struggled to force its body through the small opening. Sometime later the butterfly was still straining to free itself from the prison walls of the cocoon. Its body was only about one half outside when it stopped struggling for a bit. The man thought it had reached the end of its strength and had given up. At this point he wanted to help the exhausted butterfly. He took a small pair of scissors and made the hole in the cocoon larger so the butterfly could emerge more easily from the cocoon. When the butterfly was finally free, it had a swollen body and small shriveled up wings.

The man waited and watched expectantly. He was sure that at any moment the wings would unfold and expand in order to support the still swollen body of the butterfly. But it was never able to fly up and away. The man, in his haste to be kind, did not know how important it was for the butterfly to gain its own freedom by squeezing through the small opening in the cocoon. That struggle through the small hole in the wall of the cocoon was God's way, through the natural order, to force the fluid from the butterfly's body into the wings. That process would inflate the wings and strengthen them so the butterfly could lift itself heavenward. Because the butterfly could not fly, it could not get to a supply of nourishment and soon died.

We have all watched a small toddler struggling as it learns to walk. It is a long process as it first learns to pull its body up to a piece of furniture. This strengthens the little legs and encourages the child to try to do more. Then the child tries to take off with its first step but falls down, gets up, falls down, gets up, falls down, gets up—repeating the process until one day with wobbly hesitant legs, it struggles to take several steps before falling into the waiting arms of an encouraging parent across the room.

If the child's parents had picked it up every time it fell and put it in a safe and secure restricted place, the child would not have learned to walk when it was ready.

We are each a child of God. Is it possible that God in His infinite wisdom allows us to struggle at times so we will be strong enough to walk the way of life? He doesn't cut open our cocoons so we will have an easy way out from many of our struggles, which could leave us emotionally and spiritually crippled. We, too, might never be able to walk or fly.

To paraphrase Paul's words of encouragement to the Christians in Rome, "struggle produces endurance, endurance produces character, character produces hope, and hope never disappoints us."

Dear Father, we thank you for the inner strength You give us each day to "keep on keeping on." Amen.

Kindness Is the Badge of Love

I do not always take the time to read the letters to the editor in our daily newspaper. However, the caption on one of the letters recently caught my attention. It read: "Small Acts of Kindness Often Go Unreported." I was intrigued because reports of kind acts seldom make the news.

The letter was written by a man who observed an unexpected act of kindness when he was standing in a check-out line in a local discount department store. A young immigrant mother was buying a pair of sandals for her little girl. The check-out clerk was a teenage Asian American. The two women communicated with nods and smiles. When the clerk rang up the purchase she told the mother that she was still a dollar short, but the mother, who appeared to have offered all the money she had, did not understand. Without hesitating, the young clerk pulled a dollar from her own apron and said, "I'll get it." The mother nodded and smiled, apparently unaware of what the clerk had just done. She picked up the sandals and left the store with her happy daughter.

The letter writer, who was moved by what he had just seen, handed the young clerk a dollar bill and said, "Let me give you your dollar back." At first she refused but the man insisted and commended her for her kind act. She thanked him warmly and reluctantly accepted the dollar. As she did so, she blushed and said, "That was my lunch money."

How beautiful! There are really two acts of kindness in this story. The first good deed by the clerk generated the second thoughtful act by the gentleman who was waiting in the check-out line. That is the way it often works!

In 1 Corinthians 13, the apostle Paul gives some very powerful descriptions of the power of kindness and love. Paul was convinced that nothing in our relationships with each other is as important as love. God has shown His love to us in the most powerful manner possible through the gift of His Son whose life reveals the quality of that love for us. Paul called it God's agape love. Jesus Christ is that love personified. Agape love is the giving of oneself with no thought of return.

God gave His Son with no thought of return. Christ gave His life on the cross with no thought of return. Early Christian martyrs gave their lives with no thought of return. The young clerk gave her lunch money with no thought of return.

Surely, this must be an example of the highest kind of unselfish love we can show to one another. Our Lord was speaking about this kind of love when He said, "All will know that you are my disciples if you love one another" (John 13:35 NIV). In essence, kindness and agape love are the badges of a Christian.

Lord, Help Me Lighten Up

"A good laugh is sunshine in a house."—Thackery
"Take time to laugh, for it is the music of the soul."
"Laughter is God's sunshine."

*R*esearch has shown that when humor is used as a part of therapy, it usually speeds up recovery time. Laughter greatly reduces stress in a person and serves to increase creativity. Therapists have long recognized that a basic sense of humor and optimism along with physical laughter are good for us physically, psychologically, and spiritually.

One of the best places to begin is to laugh at yourself. Laughter does not come easily when it is painful just to make those first body movements in the morning. However, I do know that a thankful heart— "This the day which the Lord has made. I will rejoice and be glad in it."—helps me to get out of bed each morning. A thankful and joyful beginning of the day helps laughter come more easily. Someone has gone so far as to say that we each need one good laugh before breakfast. Some mornings I can't help but laugh when I first look in the mirror!

Some days "laugh starters" are delivered in our mailbox when some of the gift catalogs arrive. Humorous sayings or mottos are often painted on wall plaques or woven into gift pillows. Here are some that have "tickled my funny bone." I offer them to give you some chuckles for today.

- Greet each day with a smile and get it over with.—W. C. Fields
- Every time I see things your way, I get a headache.
- I am on a thirty-day diet. So far I've lost fifteen days.
- Give a man an inch and he thinks he is a ruler.
- The rooster crows, but the hen delivers the eggs.
- There cannot be a crisis in my life this week. My schedule is already full.
- I married Mr. Right . . . Mr. Always Right.
- A woman is like a tea bag. You never know how strong she is until she gets in hot water.—Eleanor Roosevelt
- By the time you find those green pastures, you can't climb the fence.

Dear God, You have promised to fill my mouth with laughter and my lips with shouts of joy. Please lighten up my heart so that I may live well, laugh more, and love much. Thank You, thank You, thank You, and Amen.

Please Fill My Cup, Lord

My husband has remained a bright and cheerful "morning person" during all of the fifty-five plus years we have been married. I, on the other hand, have remained a bright and cheerful "night person." I tend to shift into high gear after ten o'clock in the evening when he is ready to retire for the day. It is amazing to both of us that we have made it together for all these years.

One of the pleasures I have experienced since his retirement is that steamy cup of coffee he brings to my bedside table each morning. He knows that wonderful Colombian coffee aroma will help to pry my sleepy eyes open to begin a new day. As I savor that cup of hot coffee, some of my first conscious feelings stimulate my thanks to God for the rest that has restored me and for the new day that awaits me. Often during this quiet time the words and melodies of a familiar hymn or chorus come to mind. I recently found myself humming a chorus we had sung the day before at a Service of Holy Communion in our church.

> Fill my cup, Lord, I lift it up, Lord.
> Come and quench this thirsting of my soul.
> Bread of heaven, feed me till I want no more.
> Fill my cup, fill it up and make me whole.
>
> —Richard Blanchard

These words, of course, relate to the celebration of the Lord's Supper. However, they have an even broader meaning for me. I feel I am really asking my Lord to fill my cup—the cup that's my life—so I may become more like Him. I am asking Him to fill my cup with a deepened awareness of His presence in my life. With His help I can become a whole human being and will be able to meet life head on today. As I look back on my life, I realize that the Lord has faithfully kept my cup filled with things I have needed along the way:

- Many times it has been full and running over with refreshing joy which has reminded me how great it is just to be alive.
- Sometimes it has been filled to the brim with compassion and I was nudged to be sensitive to someone who needed special love that day.
- At other times my cup has held an extra amount of courage which enabled me to step out in faith into a new venture which changed my life.
- Frequently my cup has sparkled with beauty. I have been surprised by a special serendipity as I caught sight of the iridescent rainbow of colors on the wings of a butterfly as it flitted from blossom to blossom on our bush.
- Oftimes He has poured a soothing, healing peace into my cup when stress, anxiety, and pain were heavy in my life.
- And always, ever present, sometimes at the very bottom of my cup, I have found hope which has enabled me to try again and again.

Ah, life will always be good when we find these precious gifts which God has poured into our cup—joy, compassion, courage, beauty, peace, and hope. Our cup will never be empty if we lift it up to Him in faith. Amen and Amen!

Miracle on I-44

A man was going down from Jerusalem to Jericho, and fell . . . A Samaritan while traveling came near him . . . and when he saw him, he was moved with compassion (Luke 10:30–33 NRSV).

I have read and heard the story of the Good Samaritan many times, and have heard some very challenging sermons based on that story. However, a few months ago it had a very real and fresh impact on me when I learned of an incident which took place along one of our busy interstate highways.

A young man of college age was traveling from a northwestern state back to his home in Tennessee. Wanting to reach home as quickly as possible, he had driven too many miles without sleep or wholesome food. Due to a medication he was taking, the combination of not enough food and a lack of sleep put too much strain on his body. When he realized he was losing consciousness, he quickly pulled his SUV over to the side of the highway. In his attempt to get more fresh air and avoid blacking out completely, he got out of his car and leaned on the side of it for support.

A couple was driving home after attending their Sunday morning worship service where the scripture lesson and sermon had been based on the story of the Good Samaritan. They came upon the young man who was huddled against the side of his car and appeared to be in some kind of physical distress. In recent years the couple had refrained from helping persons along the roadside as they feared for their own safety. The husband, however, felt he must stop to help the young man who obviously needed assistance. The strong message in the morning's sermon he had just heard had stirred an unusual sense of compassion in his heart. His sensitivity to the powerful gospel story and the nudging of the Holy Spirit in his life compelled him to stop.

He walked over to the young man and immediately realized that he was ill. He helped him get into their car and rushed him to the emergency room at the local hospital. Tests were made, nourishment was given, and the young man's family was notified. Throughout this entire experience, it was evident that the husband and wife gave the same tender care to this young stranger that they would have given to one of their own three sons.

After the young man had responded to the hospital care, he was released with instructions concerning ways to help speed his recovery. The couple wanted to take him to their own home to make sure he got the necessary rest from a good night's sleep, but the young man persuaded them that he would be all right if he went to a motel. They went back to the highway, drove his SUV back into town, and made sure he was comfortably settled in his motel room before leaving him. The following morning, they returned to the motel to make sure that the young man had recovered enough to drive the remaining miles to his home.

The care and compassion of this unbelievably sensitive man and woman epitomizes the best example of modern day Good Samaritans in action. This is a true story and they are real people. The man and woman who stopped to render service are David and Brenda, and the young college student is my beloved grandson, Hart! Surely, this was a modern day miracle on a midwest interstate. Thanks be to God that the parable which Jesus told many years ago still moves His disciples to respond in love and action.

I Have Learned

At different ages and stages in life we have varying levels of awareness of our surroundings. The relative importance of particular people and things around us changes and provides new lessons as we move from the age of six to eighty-six. I was reminded of some of those insights as I read some lifetime observations which appeared in a church newsletter along with some others I have thought about or which were sent to us on the Internet. Here are some which gave me some chuckles and others which have prompted me to give more serious thought to my own life experiences.

- At age 6 I learned to love my Sunday school teacher when she cried as our class sang "Silent Night" in our children's Christmas program.
- At age 8 I quickly learned that my dog, Lucky, didn't want to eat my broccoli either.
- At age 11 I learned that when I got my room arranged the way I liked it, Mom made me straighten it up again.
- At age 15 I learned it wasn't worth cheating on a test to get better grades.
- At age 20 I learned that finding the right kind of life partner was a very crucial decision.
- At age 26 I learned that brushing my child's hair was one of life's great pleasures.

- At age 35 I learned that wherever I went, the world's worst drivers had followed me there.
- At age 39 I learned that whenever someone said unkind things about me, I needed to live so no one would believe them.
- At age 41 I learned that you can tell a lot about a man by the way he handles three things: a rainy day, lost airplane luggage, and tangled Christmas tree lights.
- At age 43 I learned that life sometimes gives you a second chance.
- At age 45 I learned that making a living was not the same thing as making a life.
- At age 50 I learned that you should not go through life with a catcher's mitt on both hands. You need to be able to throw something back.
- At age 52 I learned that children and grandparents are always on the same side when some questions arise.
- At age 55 I learned that just being there with a troubled friend was more healing than many words of advice.
- At age 60 I learned that you can make someone's day by simply sending them a caring note.
- At age 65 I learned to believe in miracles, because by then I had seen several.
- At age 68 I learned that keeping a garden was worth more than a medicine cabinet full of pills.
- At age 72 I learned that everyone at any age needs a prayer.
- At 78 I learned if you pursue happiness through life, it may elude you. But if you focus on doing the best you can, it will find you.
- At age 83 I learned I still have so much to learn.
- At age 86 I learned along with the apostle Paul to be "content with whatever I have" (Phil. 4:11 NRSV).

Let Freedom Ring!

Several years ago my husband and I visited that fascinating city of contrasts—Hong Kong. At that time it was a thriving British colony and was operating under a free enterprise system. In 1997 the ninety-nine-year British lease ended and Hong Kong reverted back to rule under the Chinese government with headquarters in Beijing. Since then there has been a "slow but sure erosion of their freedom," according to Martin Lee, one of their leading democratic legislators.

At another time, we were in Germany on the fourth of July when the dreaded Berlin wall was being constructed. Along with our German friends, we realized that movement between East and West Berlin was being "forboden." No longer would the Berliners be able to visit or conduct business with their families, friends, and associates who lived on the other side of the wall. They were living in a city which had been torn asunder.

Today, those who live in Hong Kong are struggling to maintain every form of freedom against the Beijing government. Those who live in Berlin are thriving under a new burst of freedom which came when their wall was torn down, brick-by-brick.

Webster's describes a state of freedom with such phrases as: "not controlled by others; to be physically free and to move about at will; to be mentally and politically free to embrace the ideologies we believe in." It defines slavery as "being held in bondage by another; to be owned as property and to be in service to another."

When anyone or anything controls us or possesses us against our will we are enslaved. When we are at liberty to live according to our free will and best judgment we are free. Self-imposed and self-perpetuated habits, associations, and pressures often imprison us or others whom we know. Some become slaves to the use of alcohol, tobacco, or hard drugs. Some become addicted to gambling, either legal or illegal. Some become enslaved to certain demanding relationships that smother, dictate, or dominate. Some are bound by an obsession, such as perfectionism which extends into every area of their lives. Some are captive to the cultural mores and customs in the society around them. Such entrapments always diminish the quality of life and destroy the zest for living.

I am reminded of the apostle Paul's words of encouragement to the Christians in Galatia: "Freedom is what we have—Christ has set us free! Stand, then, as free men, and do not allow yourselves to become slaves again" (5:1 GOOD NEWS). When Christ becomes the Master of our lives, He sets us free!

Dear Father, thank you for coming to us in Christ as our Liberator. Amen.

Homecoming

Thomas Wolfe once wrote that we cannot go home again. My answer to him is, "Oh, yes, you can, because I just did!" At the same time, I must also agree somewhat with Mr. Wolfe's premise. After living in other parts of the country for sixty years, I realized that going back home can never be the same because things are not the way we left them and we are not the same as when we left.

My husband and I have just returned from attending the sixtieth reunion of my high school class. Every moment was special, and there were lots of hugs and handshakes. At our age, even the men were open to some hugs. Such public demonstrations of affection were unthinkable in our community when we were in high school sixty years ago.

From our 1941 graduating class of twenty-six, fifteen of us along with a number of our spouses came back to celebrate the occasion. Five of us had come from some distance and the remainder of those present were still living in the general area, maintaining family businesses in town or on farms. All of our time together was enjoyable—from late night talks to informal chats as we watched the parade. (The town was celebrating their annual "Hubbard Days" festive weekend.) A banquet also provided an opportunity for us to catch up with one another. The annual community Sunday morning worship service in the city park brought the congregations of the town together to celebrate their common faith. Here we had a chance to greet others whom we had not seen for many years.

I grew up in this small town of about a thousand people where there was only one "Main Street" of businesses and churches of four different denominations occupied four corners during my youth. Hubbard, Iowa, has a rich German heritage and is located in an area where the soil is black and very productive. As we drove slowly up and down the streets of the town, many warm memories came to mind. Some of my reflections of our visit to my home town were:

- Main Street seemed to be narrower and shorter than it used to be;
- the "new home" my parents had built when I was in seventh grade wasn't as spacious as I remembered it;
- the school buildings which I attended from kindergarten through the twelfth grade did not seem to be nearly as large and impressive as they once had been;
- many caring people became my loving extended family for me during those years; and
- when my parents did not always know what I was doing, or where I was, someone else always did!

At the same time I was once again impressed by the progressive spirit and sense of community pride which has always been so much in evidence:

- homes are well kept with flourishing flowers and neatly maintained gardens;
- a number of new homes have been built and new neighborhoods have been developed;
- an attractive cluster of apartments have been made available for senior citizens who want to maintain independent living quarters;
- a spacious health care center has been developed for those who need continuing care;
- new churches have been built to replace older buildings and others have been remodeled; and
- new community recreational facilities now include a swimming pool, a football field, a golf course, and a clubhouse.

I was reminded that those who live and work close to God's earth develop a profound sense of gratitude and responsibility for all His gifts to them. I shall always be grateful that my roots were planted and my growing up years were cultivated in Hubbard, Iowa. I am grateful that I did go home again.

Life on Tiptoe

There are experiences in our lives which pointedly remind us of the passing of time. They cause us to remember the years gone by and to reflect on the possible years we have left to live. I have recently returned from such an event. It was the reunion of the members of my high school graduating class who had gathered to celebrate the sixtieth anniversary of our graduation in 1941.

A question lingers in my mind, "Am I really this old?" Although the courthouse records show that I am seventy-eight years old, in my mind I usually feel I am seventy-eight years young. Some days, however, my body tells me I must be over eighty-five years old. There are many things I used to do which I cannot physically do now, and I have lost interest in them. Even the psalmist wrote of his recognition of the aging process that was taking place in his life: "I have been young. Now I am old" (Ps. 37:25 NIV).

A motto on a wall plaque describes our reluctance to admit the limitations which come with the passing of years. It reads: "I'm not aging. I just need repotting!" Everyday is a precious gift from God. Life is too fleeting to let its gifts pass us by. Therefore, in this "repotting" stage of my life I need to concentrate on the activities I feel God wants me to do. They are also the acts that bring satisfaction and joy to others as well as to me. A day is always full of good vibrations when I have done something special for another person. They are not acts of heroic dimensions, but the very small things of everyday living, such as:

- taking time to talk with a neighborhood child,
- telling another person how special he or she is,
- taking a loaf of bread or a bouquet of freshly cut roses to a neighbor,
- writing a note of encouragement to someone who is ill,
- making a telephone call to someone who lives alone,
- telling some member of my family everyday how much I love them.

Alta Becker was an editor and a very special friend during the years we lived in Dayton, Ohio. We were both members of the general staff family of the Evangelical United Brethren Church. She wrote this prayer to herself and to others who were growing older along with her:

Lord, Thou knowest better than I that I am growing old. Keep me from the fatal habit of thinking that I must say something on every subject and on every occasion. Release me from craving to straighten out everyone's affairs. Make me thoughtful but not moody; helpful but not bossy. With my vast store of wisdom, it seems a pity not to use it all, but Thou knowest, Lord, that I want a few friends in the end.

Keep my mind free from the recital of endless details. Give me wings to get to the point. Seal my lips on my aches and pains. They are increasing, and the love of rehearsing them is becoming sweeter as the years go by. Help me to endure with patience the tales of another's pains. Teach me the glorious lesson that occasionally I may be mistaken.

Keep me reasonably sweet. I do not want to be a saint . . . some of them are so hard to live with. Give me the ability to see the good things in unexpected places and talents in unexpected persons. And grant me the grace to tell them so.

Keep me where I can extract all possible fun out of life. There are so many funny things in life, and I don't want to miss any of them. Amen!

Grandma Moses, who began her career as a painter when she was in her nineties, was once asked to tell the secret of her vitality. She replied, "Life is what you make it. Always has been, always will be."

For age is opportunity no less than youth itself, though in another dress. And as the evening twilight fades away, the sky is filled with stars invisible by day.

—Henry Wadsworth Longfellow

Give In or Give Up

One of life's mysteries is why some are born with strong healthy bodies, while others are forced to contend with disabilities or conditions leading to disease. Life often throws us a curveball and gives us lessons in packages we did not request or expect.

I was born with a birth defect that has plagued me throughout my life. I learned early on that there are always opportunities for growth and unexpected strength even in the midst of limitations and pain. Through the years I have come to believe that God grants us extra coping skills when life hands us "second best" physically, mentally, or emotionally. A wholesome positive sense of pride, or self-esteem, is an important part of who we are. Often, it is only that pride which enables us to try harder, to push on ahead, and to accomplish that which we didn't think was possible for us to achieve.

There are some occasions, however, when we cannot do things alone because of our limitations. In those moments we need to ask for and accept the help of others. "Giving in" by depending on others for their help can be a large and bitter pill to swallow. However, by graciously accepting assistance, we are helping others feel the joy of giving. For, "it is more blessed to give than to receive" (Acts 20:35 NRSV).

Accepting help from others is never easy, for in doing so, we lose some of our independence and are surrendering a part of our own control to others. I reached such a time in my life several years ago. Our denomination had entrusted me with a position of leadership for a program that would introduce a new concept of leadership to the women of our church. This national training program would involve many workshops and much travel back and forth across the country. At first, this appeared to be an impossibility for me.

I knew I could not make the decision alone. I had to emotionally step aside and depend on God's guidance and the advice of my family to help me choose whether or not I should undertake this responsibility. It finally came down to a "give in" or "give up" choice. Was I willing to give in and start asking and accepting help from others, or should I give up and walk away from this leadership challenge to which I believed God had called me? I knew it would require me to use wheelchairs in airports as a point of beginning. I recall the first rides weren't very comfortable as I had to depend on complete strangers to help me get to and from the planes. I soon realized that each ride became easier. It did not take many trips to convince me that the skycaps knew the shortest routes to get me to the departing gates. I learned to know them as a jolly group of fellows.

During those years I had several unusual experiences, but one stands out in my memory. My conecting flight time was tight, so in order to save time, they hoisted the wheelchair (with me in it) on the lift which the ground crew used for loading food and other supplies for the flight. Where there is a will, there is almost always someone who will think of a way.

The words of the late Catherine Marshal still come to me often when such occasions arise. She wrote, "There is great maturity in being helpless."

Through the years I have learned that my life is always enriched when I:

- keep a positive up-beat attitude;
- keep a sense of adventure;
- keep a sense of humor;
- keep a smiling countenance;
- keep open to the kindness of others; and
- keep looking for opportunities to witness to God's goodness.

Give in—Always.
Give up—Never!

Where Everybody Cares

A special call to commitment has come from the pastor of our church. He has challenged us to invite a neighbor, a friend, or someone from our office to come and share an hour of worship with us. Or—better still—we might call and make arrangements to pick up a friend or a family member and bring him or her to worship with us.

A church researcher has identified the number one reason individuals seek out a church home. It is because they feel a need to find and become related to a warm and caring fellowship. This has caused me to recall the many situations in my life when I have felt with a certainty that someone in my church cared about me and all others in our church. I have felt I was in a fellowship of love and caring when:

- I saw someone smiling at me as I entered the sanctuary;
- I felt a tender tap on my shoulder as someone entered the pew behind me;
- I realized someone was shaking my hand before I could reach for theirs;
- I saw the beautiful altar flower arrangement being dismantled after worship to be taken to the hospital or to a shut-in at home or in a health care facility;
- I heard my name being called as I was leaving the worship service and someone said they had missed me at the last circle meeting;
- I received an e-mail from a church friend asking me to pray with her about a problem in her life;

- I found my kitchen flooded with food when my mother died;
- I received a note of caring on the anniversary of her death two years later—someone had remembered;
- I learned a church member had found an anonymous cash gift in his mailbox when he had lost his job;
- I received many forms of good wishes when a new baby joined our wider family circle;
- I received a special telephone call from a church friend who just wanted to wish me a good day;
- I was joined at the hospital by a pastor and several Sunday school class friends as I waited the outcome of my husband's surgery;
- I had a phone call from a circle friend who wanted to talk about some faith questions that were troubling her;
- I found a bouquet of home-grown roses at my door even though there was no special occasion.

Just as I enjoy and appreciate being a part of a Christian community where everybody cares, I realize that I, too, must do my part to help maintain that spirit by being someone who cares for others. A Roman Catholic poet expressed that thought in this beautifully sensitive prayer poem:

The Wire Fence

The wires are holding hands around the holes;
To avoid breaking the ring, they hold tight the neighboring wrist,
And it's thus that with holes they make a fence.
Lord, there are lots of holes in my life.
There are some in the lives of my neighbors.
But if you wish, we shall hold hands,
We shall hold very tight,
And together we shall make a fine roll of fence to adorn Paradise.
—Michel Quoist

Never Enough Time

$\mathcal{J}$t was a special day of renewal and restoration for our minds and spirits as a group of us sat under the capable leadership of Gwen White in a spiritual retreat. She led us through mental exercises, periods of prayer, times of discussion and moments of complete silence. In one of our group exercises she passed a basket of slips of paper and asked each of us to take one. One word was written on each piece. She suggested that during the remainder of the day we should each ponder the meaning of the word we had drawn and how it related to our daily living.

The word I drew was "simplify." As I thought about my word, I realized how appropriate it was for me because I really did need to simplify my life. Now, several years later, that little worn slip of paper containing the word "simplify" is still posted on the door of my refrigerator. It serves as a constant reminder to me.

Simplifying our lives is not a new concern, nor is it mine alone. In a 1935 issue of *The Women's Home Companion* there is the comment that, "year by year the complexities of this world become more bewildering. Each year we need all the more to seek peace and comfort in the joyful 'simplistics' of life."

The emphasis on our need to simplify our lives has continued to dominate many current books and articles. In the nineties, articles appeared in numerous magazines ranging from the fashion conscious *Vogue* to the practical *Kiplinger's Personal Finance*. Popular books have been written on the subject: *The Circle of Simplicity, Simple Living, The Journey of Voluntary Simplicity,* and *Plain and Simple*. The latter is a sensitively written account of the simple life of an Amish family.

The need for a slower pace in our lives today is also reflected in our surroundings. In the late 1980s home builders began to design new houses with Victorian wraparound porches that remind us of days when lives moved at a slower pace and passersby would stop and chat. I am pleased that this architectural style has continued into this twenty-first century. The resurgence in popularity of the uncluttered Shaker style antique furniture is bringing premium prices at auctions across the country.

Too often the clock and the calendar control our lives. For some, life has turned into a grudging daily race toward a finish line we never seem to reach. Seldom does anything of worth reveal itself in moments of hurry and rushing about. Lives that are fragmented rather than focused will wear us out. One critic, with a touch of humor has quipped, "So what if you win the rat race! You're still a rat."

I am a listmaker, writing down the things I hope to accomplish each day. This pre-bedtime process helps me to feel organized and focused when I wake up in the morning. Unfortunately, these lists are always full and running over. I realize I should prioritize all these activities. I must evaluate all of the things that fill up my day lest they become one chaotic batch of "doings" crowding and bumping into each other. I must set boundaries on how much I can do physically. Sometimes we get so worn out from being useful that we become useless. Perhaps I must learn to use that two letter word "no" more frequently. That old Dutch adage still rings true, "The more hurrieder I go, the more behinder I get." Someone has observed that we're now living in the fast laser lane.

God needed one day a week to rest. Why do we think we are stronger than God? We also need time to recover, to regroup, and just daydream. There are times when we need to get off the noisy carousel of daily living that just keeps going round and round and round. A recent conversation with a friend indicated her frustration with the carousel pattern of her life. She said her mind was going in twenty-five different directions that morning. She cannot help but be exhausted at the end of the day if she attempts to follow all of those hurried rabbit trails. What a headache she will have! A voice on our telephone answering machine reported that a mutual friend was ill. She concluded the message with, "There cannot be another crisis this week! My schedule is already too full!"

Dr. Leonard Sweet, writer, professor, and lecturer, has coined a new word for us. He suggests we need more time to "moodle"—to be quiet long enough to sit and be with ourselves, to push away from our work, to daydream, to hear God's thoughts, whatever. Dr. Sweet says we need to balance our time to include recreation, recuperation, and rejuvenation. I need to keep reminding myself that nothing I am doing is wasted time if it helps me restore a balance in my life.

Henry David Thoreau did not set out to become the patron saint of the simple life, but that is who he became for many of us. He believed we must learn to live life deliberately. We must master the art of sauntering through life. At his Walden Pond retreat he discovered that he could live for an entire year on three dollars! Even in the nineteenth century that was an accomplishment.

We never read that Jesus hurried to do anything. Still, He accomplished all that God had sent Him to do in the length of time He was given—about thirty years in preparation and then three short years in a public ministry.

Marie Tereas suggests a simple formula for us to follow:

Each day that is given to me,
I simply divide into three.
Some time for God,
Some time for work, and
Some time for me!

Things

"Clutter, clutter everywhere and not a spot to think!" Some of the buzz words we are hearing and seeing in books and articles are: simplify, unclutter, downsize, shed, de-junk. It seems that many individuals, young and old alike, are trying to rid their lives of many of the trappings that at one time seemed so important.

At the same time we are being bombarded every day by all forms of the media which emphasize the idea that new things will give us an easier and happier life. The acquisition of more things does not bring contentment, only an increased yearning to get more and more of the latest and best things. Too often most of us are victimized by that kind of thinking. Someone has expressed it well in these words which are laced with satirical humor, "Let he who is without clutter cast the first ball of crumpled paper."

The materialistic value system of our western world has conditioned us to believe that we must always own the "status things" of today. Is it any wonder that from the global perspective, many look on us as having too many things? As we think about some of our friends in other parts of the world who live happily, we realize their lives are devoid of so many things. They find their joy in relationships with family and friends and in the world of nature around them rather than in owning many things.

Ann Morrow Lindbergh sheds some light on contented living without objects in her insightful book, *Gift from the Sea*. Once a year she left her husband and their five children at home, while she spent two weeks in retreat in complete solitude and without any form of communication with anyone. Her place of retreat was a small cottage on an uninhabited island off the east coast which could be reached only by a small boat. Her living conditions were very sparse. In that setting she quickly shed the trappings of her family home and cleared her mind of the many demands her daily round of activities placed on her. Here, where the only sounds she heard were the lapping of the waves against the shore and the songs of the birds in the trees, she was able to think and write and feel renewed.

Most of us do not have the luxury of this kind of setting, but we can cultivate the art of shedding the trappings in our daily lives that so often seem to consume us. Someone has suggested that we intentionally shut down our gadgets for twenty-four hours and unplug our lives—unplug the phone and our answering machine, disconnect the fax, disable call waiting, take the batteries out of our beeper, give our cell phone the boot, and unplug the television and radio. What would we—what could we—do with all that quiet? We just might hear that still small voice within us!

Many are making radical and drastic lifestyle changes in order to reclaim their lives. A single professisonal woman had spent much of her career climbing very high on the corporate ladder. She had a wardrobe of expensive suits and everything to go with them, including valuable jewelry. She became tired of the stress, the traffic snarls, and the constant competitive atmosphere, so she made some drastic changes. She sold her wardrobe and bought jeans and T-shirts. She exchanged her gold earrings for a pair of working gloves. Then she hired herself out as a housekeeper to her friends who were still climbing that ladder of success. At last, she said, she realized that she had reclaimed some of her life.

Sometimes these changes which are necessary to bring about a simple lifestyle are drastic, even painful at first. A young family with three small children believed very strongly in the values of a supportive family atmos-phere for their children. Therefore, they took some very radical steps. They sold their very large new home with its huge monthly mortgage payments and moved into a smaller home which they purchased mortgage-free. They sold their two luxury cars, each of which required sizable monthly payments, and bought a good used one with low mileage. This downsizing enabled the young mother to stay at home in order to care for their small children, thus eliminating the expense of daycare. They felt their decisions were best for them at this time in the lives of their three children.

Sometimes, we all need to slough off a lot of things which are no longer that important to us and tend to clutter up our homes, our garages, and our lives. Some have taken the garage sale route to do that. (Caution: garage sales can become addictive! I believe my husband would rather go to a garage sale than to a good movie or a symphony concert.) An ad in our local paper read:

> We are simplifying our lives. Won't you help us by coming by 601 West Main Street for our Friday evening twilight sale beginning at 6 P.M. and continuing through Saturday? We will be selling some choice antiques, good clothing, lawn and garden supplies, and a lot of really good junque.

That may be one good way to begin uncluttering our lives. To simplify our lives does not require that we give our new car away and canoe to work, but it does require us to decide what is really important and does not overburden us. Charles Spurgeon, a great preacher of the last century, once said, "It is not how much we have, but how much we enjoy what we have, that gives us happiness."

One day when Jesus was speaking to the people who had crowded around Him, a man asked Jesus to help settle a quarrel concerning the division of their family estate. Jesus told the man that He had not come to be a judge in such matters. However, Jesus did make a comment which is particularly relevant for us today. He said, "Take care! Be on your guard against all kinds of greed; for one's life does not consist in the abundance of possessions" (Luke 12:15 NRSV).

God's Little Interruptions

God's Little Interruptions

*W*e all live with interruptions everyday. My doorbell rings and the buzzer on my clothes dryer has just gone off, reminding me that I must take out my husband's dress shirts before they are wrinkled. Later, I hear the shrill persistent ring of the telephone over the whirring sound of my mixer as I prepare my family's favorite bran muffin recipe. Still later there is a tap, tap, tap on my backdoor just as the insistent buzzer on my oven sounds off to tell me those muffins must be taken out of the oven before they burn.

Interruptions . . . interruptions . . . interruptions. . . . They are a real part of many of my days. However, experience has taught me that often these are God's very important little interruptions breaking into my scheduled routine. We make our lists of "things to do." Our day-timers are blurry with appointments and events. The clock and the calendar have become our ruling taskmasters.

I like to think I am an organized person. Before going to bed at night I mentally organize the tasks I hope to accomplish the next day. I even write them down in the order of their importance. Somehow, my days never fall into place quite like I have planned them. God, through those halts in my days, pulls me out of my comfortably ordered cocoon. It seems He knows I may get mired down in the many mundane tasks which sometimes make me apathetic to the needs of those around me.

When Christ was encouraging the disciples to be aware of and respond to the needs of those around them, He said, "Just as you did it to one of the least of these who are members of my family, you did it to me" (Matt. 25:40 NRSV).

In this Lenten season we should allow time for God's special interruptions in our faith journey. During the forty days of Lent, Christ invites us to join Him in the spirit of His own forty days of searching and preparation. For us, this can be a time for digging out the corners of our lives as we examine our souls. This is a time when our hungry hearts can ask Him to come in and fill those empty spaces with His caring love.

Apathy is a deadly virus that can cause our hearts to harden and calcify. Lent is a time for sealing off the seams of our selfishness and a time for breaking free from the grip of our apathy. We hear this challenge dramatically and poignantly expressed in G. Studder-Kennedy's poem:

When Jesus came to Golgotha, they hanged Him on a tree,
They drove great nails through hands and feet and made a
    Calvary;
They crowned Him with a crown of thorns, red were His wounds
    and deep.
For those were crude and cruel days, and human flesh was cheap.

When Jesus came in modern day, they simply passed Him by,
They never hurt a hair of Him, they only let Him die;
For men have grown more tender, and they would never give Him
    pain,
They just passed down the street and left Him in the rain.

Still Jesus cried, "Forgive them, for they know not what they do."
And still it rained the winter rain that drenched Him through and
    through;
The crowd went home and left the streets without a soul to see,
And Jesus crouched against a wall and cried for Calvary.

Our Lenten Rose

We have a precious flower in our garden. It is the Lenten rose, a member of the Helleborus family. The flower bed where the Lenten rose is planted is near our deck and very close to the house. I can see the large clumps of green plants from the window by my desk where I work every day.

In the fall season when the days grow shorter, the leaves of autumn drop and blow away. Wintertime sets in and everything in the garden is brown and quietly rests. However, the large leaves of the Lenten rose remain perky, upright, and green.

Early in January we see the first delicate tight white buds forming under the protection of the large overhanging leaves. We watch and wait as the buds begin to swell, then lift their heads high, and finally begin to open their petals hesitantly to the light. They are like no other flower, and they are beautiful! As the blossoms finally open wide the petals are a soft spring green on ivory which shade into delicate tones of lavender at the edges. A minutia of fragile lighter green stamens lifting their delicate tendrils outward form a cluster at the center of the flower. They herald the message of spring, of new life, and of the coming of warm sunshine on this dark chilly winter day.

Each one of us passes through dark days and dark nights within our soul. Even as I write these words, I am in the throes of such a day. Today, my husband has picked one of the Lenten roses and I have placed it in a small vase on my desk. As I sit and study this delicate flower I realize that my life, too, is a tenuous fragile thing. At the same time, the beautiful blossom reminds me that there is also beauty and sunshine and joy in my life. Every day I must search to maintain that balance. My faith in Jesus Christ helps me find and sustain that harmony.

I am told that the rose in all its many forms is a German symbol for Christ. An old Arabian tale, according to German custom, tells of all the roses in the world blooming the night Jesus was born. Just as the Lenten rose is a prelude in the midst of winter of the springtime to come, so Jesus Christ, whose resurrection we celebrate on Easter morn, is a symbol of the springtime of our new life in Christ each day.

Thank You, God, for this precious Lenten rose. Thank You, Father, for sending Jesus Christ who has promised us everlasting life with You beginning today. Amen.

A Special Place

A friend sent me an interesting news clipping about Mary Engelbreit, who is the creator of a popular line of gifts and a series of whimsical greeting cards. Several years ago she designed a card bearing the message, "Everyone needs their own spot." She was amazed by the volume of mail this message generated. Some told her she had made them aware of their own need for a special place. Several of the writers told her of the unique places in which they had created a quiet corner for themselves. For one person, it was an empty closet with a shelf to hold a book and a candle for reading and a small low bench for praying. Another, who lived in a sunny clime, had a spot in her garden where the bending branches of the trees above formed an open avenue upward to the sky.

I have two quiet corners that are special places for me in our home. One is at my desk alongside a window which reaches to the floor. Through this window I can see the many birds as they fly to and from our feeders and dine on the seeds we have placed there. God has often spoken to me through the habits and activities of the birds, so I have come to expect His voice in that corner of our den. My second quiet corner is a spot in our bedroom. There is an easy chair with a pillow for my back, a footstool under my feet, and a large bay window which looks out to my world on our quiet street.

One of the quiet places to which Jesus retired was the wilderness where He spent forty days in solitude. Surely He spent countless hours in prayer with His heavenly Father. This time of quiet preparation helped

Him withstand the three wily temptations that the devil used in his effort to destroy Jesus.

Lent should be the ideal time in our spiritual year when we regularly create our own quiet place where we can listen to God in solitude. Lent is a special time for introspection as we look deep within ourselves and seek God's forgiveness for those things we have done that have separated us from Him. It is a special time to prepare ourselves to experience a fuller meaning of the resurrection which we celebrate at Easter. Lent is a special time when you and I may meet God in our quiet places.

Stuff

Our lives are full of stuff. Every spring about this time I get the urge to start stirring in my stuff. There is closet stuff, pantry stuff, cupboard stuff, drawer stuff, attic stuff, and lots of garage stuff.

I separate the good useful stuff from the not-so-good and not-so-useful stuff. Then I stuff the not-so-good and not-so-useful stuff in places where it will not be so noticeable and so much in the way. I'll decide later if I will ever need that extra stuff again. Then there is that stuff which I could not give up last year, but must get out of the way this year. But, wait, should I really do that this year? It's still good. . . .

As I sort some of the stuff, I feel that I should be adding another room, or at least another closet to hold it all. For instance, there is that too-small clothing stuff which is too good to give or throw away just now, perchance I might someday shed the extra stuff on my waist and hips. Then that clothing stuff would be useful stuff and I could wear it again.

Recently, when I felt like sorting stuff I tackled our bedroom and bath stuff. Here there was stuff to make me smell better, stuff to make me look younger, stuff to help me sleep better, stuff to help me feel better, stuff to hold me in, and stuff to give me a lift. Surely, our lives are overstuffed; some necessary and good and some not so necessary and not so good; some in good condition and some worn out and just plain junky. There is stuff everywhere and more stuff . . . stuff . . . stuff.

It is not only spring cleaning time for me. It is time to make my Lenten journey. This journey will afford hours for me to have a very special walk in God's presence; a time when He will help me sort out and get rid of some of the "shallow stuff" in my life. It will also be a time to fill my life with the "better stuff" such as the disciplines of prayer, meditation, study, and worship. This better stuff will equip me to be of more service to Him and others both now and in the days to come. Then, on Easter morn, I will claim again His promise that we may have the wonderful stuff that He has prepared for those of us who believe in Him. Hallelujah!

The Fragrance of Spring

The Fragrance of Spring

After the winter's cold slumbering months, the earth was gradually showing signs that new life was breaking through in every direction. I wanted to bring some of the spring air inside as I opened a window here and there. As the lighter fresh air began to filter into each room, everything seemed to be rejuvenated.

Up and down our street clusters of black bulging plastic bags stood like sentinels of spring as they announced to passersby that clean-up time had arrived. The working hum of a lawn mower could be heard now and then bringing with it that pungent fragrance of newly mown grass.

This reminded me that other neighbors on other streets were busy raking, trimming, mowing, and uncovering their beds of sleepy perennials. Our next door neighbor, a school principal, spent much of his spring break trimming the irregular ragged lower branches from the many trees in his yard. He piled them streetside in a neat brushpile along his driveway awaiting the chipper truck which would come along to chop them into small pieces and haul them away.

One morning, a week or so later, as I sat in my "quiet place" where I read, ponder, and pray, a fluttering movement caught my attention. As I turned to focus my attention more sharply, the fluttering stopped. Then I saw a brilliant red cardinal land on the highest twig of the huge brush pile. He was adorned in his most brilliant spring plumage in order to attract a mate for the summer and raise a family in the weeks ahead.

In contrast to the brilliance of the cardinal, the leaves on the branches were curling and twisting in the heat of the sun. As they dried they lost their color, and their dull appearance now indicated they were no longer alive.

What a symbolic image nature gave me at that special moment! It has stayed with me ever since that morning during Holy Week. Those fading, withering, dying leaves and branches represented to me the sense of sadness and sorrow we experience as we relive the events during the final week in the life of our Lord. Then suddenly there was the flash of brilliant color as that beautiful red cardinal, dressed in his brightest spring plumage, came onto the scene. He reminded me of the glory of the resurrection and the promise of eternal life which was proclaimed to the whole world on Easter morn.

And so it is for you and me. Jesus Christ died and paid the ransom for our sins. But that was not the end. The women found an empty tomb but heard a voice speaking to comfort them in the garden. Because Christ lives we may live in fellowship with Him and other believers now and on through all eternity. Alleluia!

Potential, Promise, Presence

$\mathcal{N}$atalie Sleeth has penned these words and the music to the beautiful "Hymn of Promise:"

In the bulb there is a flower,
In the seed an apple tree;
In cocoons a hidden promise
Butterflies will soon be free!
In the cold and snow of winter
There's a spring that waits to be
Unrevealed until its season
God alone can see.

A challenging writer, Sarah Ban Breathnach has titled one of her books *Something More*. In various ways she points out that we are all on a spiritual pilgrimage throughout our lifetime to search and become something more.

One of the greatest gifts God has planted deep within our being is the potential to become something more than we are. He gives to us the will and the raw materials to grow into something more than we are on any given day. God plants deep within us the desire to dredge deeper, stretch farther, and reach higher as we define and refine the miracle of who we are.

Perhaps there is no greater visible promise of "something more" than we see in a dull, lifeless, brown, peeling bulb. We plant them in our favorite decorative pots in the late fall believing that in a few weeks we will have the delicate, white, fragrant blooms of the narcissus (paper whites) to adorn our homes during the Christmas season. We plant other brown bulbs in our gardens at the same time believing that in a few months we will enjoy the bright colors of the crocus, the hyacinths, and the daffodills and other lovely heralds of spring. A motto on a little marker in our garden reads: "To plant a garden is to believe in a God of tomorrows."

Again, let us note these words of promise from the hymn by Natalie Sleeth:

There's a song in every silence,
Seeking word and melody,
There's a dawn in every darkness
Bringing hope to you and me.

Life is sometimes a series of starts, slowdowns, and stops. At times, when an important part of creative expression is shut down in one's life, a painful sense of loss floods into the vacuum that forms. Some of the sparkle and joy of each day is gone. This happened to me some years ago when my active participation in my vocation in music was taken away due to health problems. It was then that God's abiding presence in my life through the Holy Spirit often whispered, "Dredge deeper, stretch farther, and reach higher."

Eventually, I found another tiny seed that God had planted deep within me, but one which I had never cultivated. There was a pen in my hand and I found I could creatively express myself through words as well as through musical notes. And that, my friend, is the message of Easter. From the darkness of Golgotha to the dawn of the resurrection in a garden, Christ promises us the abundant life. He holds out the eternal hope of something more!

We must claim the promise by straining forward to what lies ahead as we press on toward the goal for the prize of the heavenly call of God which comes to us through Jesus Christ (Phil. 3:13–14 paraphrased).

O God, help us to claim the promise of your presence where you have planted us, in order that we might bloom with an inward and outward beauty. Amen.

Put On Joy!

*T*his is surely the season in God's natural world when He clothes His creation in full blown joy! This beautiful time of blooming helps us extend the miracle of Easter morning into Eastertide and enables us to continue nurturing the heartbeat of joy within us.

When I think about joy I realize that I often experience several kinds, each of which carries its own unique delightful excitement. One of the special joys in my life is the "joy of expectancy." The joy of expectancy fills my life and thoughts as I anticipate each new day, with each special occasion as I think about it and plan for it.

In the springtime I always feel the joy of expectancy when I think about the first blush on the redbud trees and the beautiful snowy white blossoms of the dogwood. It was Goethe, the German poet, who challenged his readers to: "Live each day as if your life has just begun."

I have labeled another kind of joy in my life "joy from the inside out." This joy is rooted in and nurtured when I practice daily spiritual disciplines. I know this joy when I spend moments of the day with our Lord. This joy nestles in my heart as I read and ponder the words in my Bible, as I study the writings of other inspired writers, as I pray, and as I earnestly listen for God's voice to me throughout the day. It is then that the joy in my heart breaks out from the inside and permeates each hour of my day.

"Joy in relationships" is a theme which runs through the life of the person who likes to be with others. Adam was lonely so God gave him a companion. How desolate and lonely our lives would be if we knew and associated only with those in our household. Emotions, ambition, and goals in life are played out against a background of our relationships with many others. We are reminded of the meaningful relationships among the early first century Christians when an outsider commented, "See how these Christians love each other."

When difficulties seem to be overwhelming, a fresh awareness of God's presence in my life has a soothing and calming effect which enables me to cope with any difficulty that a day may bring. I call this soul refreshment my "joy in spite of. . . ."

For many months *Tuesdays with Morrie* was on the *New York Times* non-fiction best-seller booklist. It is the remarkable account of a series of conversations between a student and his brilliant former college professor, Morrie, who was stricken with a progressive degenerative disease for which there was no cure. At one point, Morrie was asked how he was doing. His confident reply was, "I am determined that nothing will ever take away my joy."

While imprisoned by the Nazis and awaiting the hangman's noose, the late German theologian, Dietrich Bonhofer, expressed his conviction that we should be grateful (and joyful) even when there is no great spiritual experience. Further, he believed that we should always "be looking forward eagerly for the highest good." He knew and experienced "joy in spite of. . . ."

At the end of a long day I often feel "joy overflowing." I thank God that He has given me another day with its bright moments. I rest in His everlasting arms in the knowledge that I am His beloved child. Often my last thoughts of the day are a prayer of thanksgiving and a question, "How can I be this happy?" The answer comes quickly. Jesus assured His disciples that His joy is available for the asking (John 16:24). Our God is a joyful God, and He invites us to put on His joy.

From the pen of Donna Swanson come these beautiful thoughts about joy:

> Joy came walking on silent feet surprising my heart with its laughter.
> It danced in the eyes of my children and spilled from the heart of my husband.
> It jumped up from the pages of a book and reached out through the touch of a friend.

While weary with the pilgrimage through a dark and lonely
country,
I found it as a rippling, curling stream running lightly over the
troubled stones.
And I knew, as I sensed its fullness, that this joy was the laughter
of God.

May the Lord bless you and keep you going with joy!

Two Arms Crossed for Us

Psychologists remind us that occasionally we need to take some time from our scheduled routines to do something that is enjoyable for us, something that refreshes—a mini-vacation—during the day. This past week I did just that. I went to the hall closet where we store symbols of our seasonal memories. I unpacked several treasures which are appropriate for this springtime Easter season. Now standing on the lazy susan on our kitchen table is a small, strange-looking, aqua-colored pottery rabbit. His ears do not match and he sports an off-center button shaped tail. This strange little creature was made by our daughter, Suzanne, when she was an eight-year-old member of a Brownie troop. Standing alongside that bunny there is a little pink rabbit holding her baby in her arms. Originally this little rabbit was pretty with coy downcast eyes showing her long lashes. However, the years of moving from one house to another have taken their toll on her pottery body. It is evident that both ears have been broken and glued back in place. The surface of an arm is crazed and there is a deep white chip showing at the bottom of her skirt. Neither of the bunnies is perfect, however, they are both special to me. I have placed them in the same place on our kitchen table for more than forty years and they continue to bring back feelings of warm and happy memories.

During the years that we have lived in the South we have added other special things to our family traditions and springtime customs. Each year I have enjoyed arranging bouquets of dogwood blossoms and placing them in different locations in our home. This year I placed a mixed bouquet of red and white blossoms in our foyer. They brought back happy memories of our daughter's April wedding years ago when I decorated our entire home with them.

Every year as I arrange them I remember the age-old legend about the dogwood tree. The dogwood trees once grew tall and straight, and were generally used for making posts and beams. One year evil men used two pieces of wood to make the cross on which our Lord was crucified. According to the legend, they were straight limbs from a dogwood tree. Forever after that time, the native dogwood trees have been twisted and bent. As I looked on those blossoms I was reminded of my emotions last Sunday as I entered the sanctuary of our church for worship. The elegant spacious beauty of the sanctuary inspired me. Rich symbols of traditions and meaning were everywhere. As I sat in our pew for my quiet moments my gaze was drawn to "it." There in stark relief against the plain high wall to the left of the pulpit stood a heavy rough hewn wooden cross. It was at least fifteen feet tall and was based in a mound of large irregular rocks. Ropes were entwined around the beams where they intersected to form the cross. My initial feeling was one of shock. My eyes filled with tears. Of course, the cross must have a central place in the church, but not this dark heavy one. I realized I was more comfortable looking at the bright and shiny brass cross on the communion table, not this ugly reminder of Good Friday's suffering.

God did create "all things bright and beautiful." Only man would make a cross out of beams he had cut from a tree of beauty. God transformed that symbol of shame into a symbol of the salvation he offers to each of us through faith in the Christ who hung there. The commercialization of the world around us at Easter would "squeeze us into its own mold," but that can happen only if we allow it.

- Because of Golgotha's ugly cross we can celebrate the empty cross!
- Because Christ suffered on that ugly cross we can have the abundant life here and now!
- Because Christ gave his life on that ugly cross, we can have eternal life with Him forever!

So, with all the saints we sing at Eastertime "In the Cross of Christ We Glory!"

Autumn's Last Smile

Autumn's Last Smile

*A*utumn is perhaps my favorite season of the year. William Bryant captured the feeling of this special time when he wrote, "Autumn—the year's last loveliest smile."

Many of us have lived in climates where winter brings dark gray days. Their monotonous moods seem endless when the dreary clouds laden with heavy snows come to hover over us and settle in for months. It is small wonder that in these corners of our country autumn days are so treasured and so precious.

We have just returned from our annual trek to New England. Ah, our favorite New England and such golden days with:

- bright blue October skies;
- crisp mornings when the first frosts of the season leave sparkling diamond crystals on our car;
- mid-day sun so warm, bidding us to savor the day; and
- evenings sharp and snappy reminding us to reach for our sweaters and jackets.

Again this year, we drove down those special country roads that promise a surprise around each bend. We felt closed in snugly by the fiery red maples and the stately straight pines accented by the thin white stripes of the birches on both sides of the road.

Along these quiet roads we saw preparations which reminded us that those "loveliest smiles of autumn" would soon be gone for this year. There were wood piles in many yards—some still waiting to be split, and others which had already been stacked. We occasionally saw evidences that some of that wood was already being used to take off the morning chill as blue smoke came out of the chimneys in straight frothy signals like feathery plumes up into a blue windless sky. Oh, what a heavenly fragrance!

As we drove through the quiet villages and towns, we saw bright shining red snowmobiles lined up in rows behind large "For Sale" signs. These heralded the days when drifting snow would soon cover many trails and roads as well as the highways.

On one particularly crisp morning we stopped at a roadside restaurant for a cup of coffee and a roll. I overheard another customer say to our waitress, "I'm not putting on my heavy jacket yet. (Even though she appeared to be a bit chilly.) Once it goes on, it will be months before it comes off." These weather-wise New Englanders were reminding us that even as we were enjoying the last smile of autumn, the winter days were coming soon.

The bountiful beauty all around us which changes with the passing of each season reminds us of God's constancy in the natural order. God is present in the warm autumn days as well as in the winter days when the wind blows and the snows drift across the road. And so it is as we live out our lives. God is equally present in the changing emotional and spiritual seasons of our souls.

Sometimes we seem to be de-sensitized to all of the physical beauty around us as we tend to live in the "fast lanes" of life. Sometimes we fail to acknowledge the beauty and joy to be found in our relationships with others as we live by the incessant ticking of the clock.

On that lovely ride through the beautiful New England countryside, my husband and I realized anew that we are living in the autumn years of our lives. We have each lived more years than we have left. We agreed we should make every moment and every day count. We agreed that we should be more intentional about cherishing and nurturing all our relationships, whether they be with family or with friends. In those ways, we will help fill our autumn years with the loveliest smiles of our lives.

Have you hugged someone today?

Have you told someone today that you love them?

The Secret to Contentment

Opportunities to visit with our daughter do not occur as frequently as we would like, for she lives some distance from us in another city. Recently when she was in our city on a business trip she spent several evenings with us. One evening she shared a thought that had become special to her during her devotional times that week. She said, "I have realized that one of the special blessings God has given me is that I am a contented person."

This Thanksgiving season has prompted me to reflect often on her statement. As I pondered her words I asked myself, "What does contentment mean to me and what does it bring into my life?" I have concluded that, for me, contentment brings happiness, ease of mind, a state of well-being, and a sense of peace.

A friend shared this verse by an unknown author with me:

As I was wandering o'er the green
Not knowing where I went,
By chance I saw a pleasant scene
'Twas was the cottage of content.

The culture around us strives to stimulate us to want more, more, more. Perhaps we should shift our attention away from things that we do not have to the abundance of things that we do have.

A contented heart seldom comes from an abundance of external things. A contented heart stems from a grateful heart. Each day of our life should be lived with an "attitude of gratitude." The secret of contentment is the realization that life is a gift not a right.

- Upon awakening each morning, I am grateful that God has given me another day of life. With the psalmist I will say, "This is the day the Lord has made. I will rejoice and be glad in it" (Ps. 118:24).
- I am grateful that there is enough food in my house today to nourish my physical body.
- I am grateful for the beauty in all of God's creation. As I write, I am looking at a fiery maple tree showing off its glorious colors outside my window.
- I am grateful for meaningful things to do today and for the little serendipities of joy which the day will bring in my relationships with others.
- I am grateful for the quiet moments I will find to be with God today as I listen to Him and talk with Him. Being at peace with oneself is the direct result of finding peace with God.
- I am grateful that I can take care of myself today or, if not, for the persons who stand by to help me.
- And, then, at the close of the day, I will be thankful for a safe place to anticipate a refreshing night's rest.

As we gather all of these crumbs of gratitude, let us be thankful for the smallest crumb; for all together they will bring us a loaf of contentment. Then we can say with the apostle Paul, "I have learned to be content with whatever I have" (Phil. 4:11b).

How Do You Spend These Gifts?

*I*n this season that beckons us to give thanks for all that God has given us to use and enjoy, I find myself pondering a disturbing question. "Am I a good steward of all God's gifts to me?"

One of the greatest gifts He gives to us is one which we so easily take for granted—the gift of time. We are each given an equal amount of time. We each have exactly twenty-four hours to spend each day. Another great gift from God is our freedom to make choices. God did not create us as robots. Therefore, He has given to each of us the freedom to choose how we spend each twenty-four-hour block of time.

A recent study has calculated that we spend eight months of our lives opening junk mail. That is 5,760 hours of non-essential activity. The author of the study also estimated that we spend 8,640 hours looking for misplaced objects and, as we grow older, those hours add up faster. We spend 17,820 hours trying to call individuals who are not home or whose phone lines are busy.

The report goes on to say that we are too stressed to attempt to slow down unless our bodies do the stopping for us. Balance comes only when we make the time to discover who we really are, what kind of person we want to be, and what our real life priorities should be. The researcher further suggests that we keep an hourly record of what we do every day and notice how little time we actually spend watching birds, following cloud patterns, or just day-dreaming.

I was so blessed in my growing up years to have had a great-grandmother until I was eighteen years old and both of my grandmothers for many years after I was married. I realize that their lives were less complicated than mine, but they always had relaxing hours to spend with me when I went to visit them as a child and as a youth. They always seemed to have their "work done." I recall happy summer visits with one grandmother when we would spend evening hours swinging together on her front porch. A tall mock orange bush nearby gave a heady sweet fragrance as we rocked and talked.

As I relived those special memories, my mind jumped ahead to another time in my life. My husband was in his first pastorate in a small rural church in the Midwest. He not only served as the pastor, but as a couple we were the janitors, the choir director, Sunday school teachers, the office secretary, and the groundskeeper. Our daughter was born during the first busy year when we found ourselves in all those new roles. I deeply regret that I did not make more time to read to her, to play with her, and just enjoy her then and in the busy years which followed. But the times we did spend together were always very special for us.

The years passed and we were blessed with two special grandchildren, Amy and Hart, who were born four years apart. Those were also very busy years, but we had grown wiser and we made time to spend hours with them in our home when they were babies, toddlers, and on through their youth. After they were old enough to enjoy travel, we planned special summer trips with each child separately, going to places of special interest to each of them at their particular age.

A little sign on my refrigerator expresses it well: "Grandchildren are spoiled here with love!" Their frequent visits with us and their phone calls now as young adults add to our beautiful memory bank. We are thankful that we made time for them during their crucial formative years. Now they enrich our lives so much.

How grateful I am to trace five generations of people who have enriched my life because they have given their time to me—my great-grandmother, my two grandmothers, my mother, my daughter, and my two grandchildren.

I am becoming more aware of the fact that as we use God's gift of time to nurture meaningful relationships with others we are blessed with joy, fulfillment, and contentment. Time is fleeting and I am determined to cherish each precious moment today as a gift from God. Let our lives be our thanksgiving. Let our prayers become our deeds.

Thank you, Lord, for Your great gifts to us—the gift of life, the gift of time, and the freedom to spend them as we choose. Thank You! Thank You!

Will Your Heart
Be Ready for Christmas?

Will Your Heart Be Ready for Christmas?

*A*dvent is a season of joyful expectancy. It is a time of waiting for a wonderful event that we relive every year as we look forward to God's greatest gift the world has ever known.

Perhaps one of the most positive forces in the lives of the overtaxed and downtrodden Hebrew people was their hopeful expectancy. They clung desperately to the fragile thread of promise that one day their Messiah would come. They also believed that when he did come the heels of the heavy boots of the Roman world would be lifted from their weary backs. This hopeful expectancy sustained them year after year as they waited and watched for him.

One of the special hymns we sing during the early weeks of Advent reminds us of their plight and their expectation.

O come, O come, Emmanuel,
And ransom captive Israel
That mourns in lonely exile here
Until the son of God appears.

Come, thou long expected Jesus
Born to set Thy people free

Israel's strength and consolation
Hope of all the earth Thou art.

In all of life, expectancy always implies planning and preparation. There is always such expectant joy in the anticipation time before a wedding. But there surely must be detailed preparation if there is to be a beautiful and meaningful ceremony. When a pregnant couple celebrates their new joy about a coming baby, there surely must be a time of preparation—a nursery, baby clothes, and especially the emotional and mental preparation for the inevitable change in their lifestyle that this little baby will bring. So, too, these Advent weeks should be a time when we prepare our souls for the Christ child.

In 1968 the Christmas card which we wrote and shared with our family and friends contained these words:

'Midst all of the hustle and bustle
The hurrying to and fro
From the carols, the candles, the cookies
To the magic of twinkling lights in the snow—
Friend, please stop just a moment and ponder
Through all this hurry and fuss.
From your first to your last preparation
Are you getting your heart ready for Christmas?

Are you giving more thought
to new clothes for the many parties
or to the swaddling clothes He wore?
to the unique gift for the one who has everything
or to the gift of a shepherd boy who had nothing?
to the aroma of fruitcake and cookies
or to the fragrance of a Wise Man's incense?
to the right sized and perfectly shaped tree
or the cruel, crude tree from which He later hung?

Let us take time even now in these moments
When there are many things still to be done.
Oh, do not neglect your heart's preparation
So, that you might receive God's Christmas gift, His Son!

During these days of Advent, let us each make and take time each day for some moments of calm and quiet just to be with God. Such moments can be prayerfully wedged in between the cracks of our busyness. Perhaps then, when you and I celebrate the birth of Jesus, the Christ Child, on Christmas Eve we will be better prepared to fling open the doors of our hearts to welcome Christ into our lives more completely.

Dear Father, help us to attend to our little errands of love early this year so that the brief days before Christmas may be unhampered and clear of the fever of hurry. Save us from the breathless rushing that we have known in the past. Grant us a calm serenity in our soul. Amen.

Who Was She?

*T*o many of her neighbors she was probably not that unusual. They saw her as an ordinary teenage peasant girl living a simple life with her parents. Some scholars believe that her parents were a bit older than the average age of parents of early teenagers. Her father's name was Joachim and her mother's name was Anne. They lived in the little village of Nazareth. By all accounts she was just an ordinary girl growing up in a small town.

Most Biblical scholars believe that Mary was about thirteen or fourteen years old. It was the custom in those days for young girls to be engaged for several years to men who were a bit older than they were. This was to allow time for the man to become established in an occupation which would enable him to support a wife and children.

While most of those who knew Mary considered her to be very ordinary, she was also known to be deeply committed to the Jewish faith of her parents and her ancestors before her. She was a naive and innocent girl who was pure as a virgin. One day God unexpectedly interrupted Mary's life when the angel Gabriel came to her and told her that God had chosen her to bear an unusual son. This son would be called the Son of God and would be the vessel through whom God would break in upon the world.

We can't possibly imagine Mary's perplexed feelings of anxiety, fear, and awe when the angel Gabriel appeared and told her what God wanted her to do for Him. Even though she did not fully understand what it was that God was asking her to do, she was faithful and totally willing and obedient to His call. Because she responded as she did to His call, God made her into an extra-ordinary person who would be known for her faithfulness through all the centuries to come.

Throughout our lifetime, I believe God calls each of us from time to time to assist Him with His plans for those about us and for our world. There will be occasions when we, like Mary, may feel that we are just very ordinary persons and may not fully understand exactly what He wants us to be or to do. But if we respond in faithful obedience, He will use us and transform us from being just ordinary persons into extra-ordinary persons—faithful children of the Most High. For we do believe that all things are possible with Him!

The Good Innkeeper

The Good Innkeeper

*T*he birth of Jesus is one of the most important events of all the New Testament stories. However, the account of this happening is found in only two of the four Gospels—Matthew and Luke.

It is Matthew who tells us that Joseph was of the royal line of David. Matthew also tells of the angel's appearance to Joseph when he was told of Mary's miraculous pregnancy and what her son would mean to the world. This writer then describes the long journey of the wisemen who followed the new star in search of the One whose birth had been foretold.

Luke devotes only six verses to the telling of this unusual story. His words are much more intimate and specific. This narrative form might be expected from a physician such as Luke. He lifts up the story of Mary's important role in the Christmas drama in a very warm and personal manner. Some scholars believe that Dr. Luke may have had a personal conversation with Mary at a later time in her life. It is only Luke who reported that "Mary treasured all these words and pondered them in her heart." Perhaps she, herself, had told him that. It is even possible that he may have served as the family physician for several other members of her large family.

It is an interesting phenomenon that we often read factual accounts and then "fill in the cracks" as we put ideas together and form a neat composite account of an event. Such is the case with the Christmas story. From our earliest childhood we have witnessed the pageants in our churches in which members of the congregation have reenacted this event. We remember:

- the shepherds with their shabby burlap garb and their shepherd crooks;
- the angel choirs with their tinseled wings and the sparkling garlands in their hair, and;
- the wisemen, wearing assorted bathrobes topped off with paper crowns that had been sprayed with gold gilt paint and carrying boxes which represented the costly gifts as they all walked down the aisles of our churches to pay homage to the Baby Jesus in a crude manger filled with straw.

Luke tells us that the shepherds did come quickly in search of the child as soon as they heard the startling message from the angels. However, the wisemen didn't arrive in Bethlehem immediately because they came from a distance. It was at least two weeks and possibly as long as two months, or even two years later. They found the child, no longer in the manger, but living elsewhere with Mary and Joseph in Bethlehem.

Let us go back again to that crowded little town in Judea which was shrouded in darkness. A jostling crowd of people and animals were pushing ahead of one another to find a place to lie down and rest after long and wearisome days on the winding dusty roads.

Sometime earlier the Roman officials had declared that every man must return to the town of his ancestors to register for a census. The Romans had become concerned about the rapidly increasing Jewish population and the urgent need to increase tax revenues. They had no other way to get an accurate head count of all those individuals, both Gentiles and Jews, who lived in the area under the Roman command.

This new decree meant that Mary and Joseph would have to make the long eighty mile trip south from their little town of Nazareth in Galilee to Bethlehem in Judea because Joseph's ancestoral home was there. Bethlehem was a very small surburban village near Jerusalem. Very likely, the more prosperous citizens traveled to Bethlehem on swift horses or in carriages. But the common people, like Joseph and Mary, made the journey with a farm animal or on foot.

Travelers of that day did not have a toll-free number to call and make advance reservations, so the limited overnight accommodations were probably assigned on a first come first serve basis. It was not surprising that Mary and Joseph were greeted with a "no vacancy" sign when they reached the village inn that night. We have usually assumed that the owner served as the caretaker and manager of the inn or large boarding house. It was customary to house the animals of the travelers in cave-like enclosures under the sleeping quarters. The heat thrown off by the animals helped take the chill off the rooms above.

Through the years we have given the innkeeper a hard time. While there is no mention in Luke's Gospel of that phantom figure, Christians have nevertheless been inclined to deal very harshly with him and have even accused him of turning Mary and Joseph away. Luke simply reported the fact that "there was no room for them in the inn." Some have criticized the innkeeper for not routing out another couple from their sleeping area to make room for Mary to deliver her baby in more comfortable quarters. But would that have been fair to the travellers who had arrived first?

Let us not forget that the innkeeper did not turn them away. He gave them the best he had! He took them to a warm place near the animals which was a private and quiet location apart from the noise of the street. I like to think of him as a tender-hearted and compassionate innkeeper. He did a very ordinary thing because he cared and God made it very extra-ordinary.

Immanuel, God is With Us!

Do You Believe in Angels?

*D*o you believe in angels? In recent years there has been a growing interest in the phenomenon of angels. The word "angel" is used in the Bible to refer to a spiritual being separate from God and of a higher order than we are. In the early days of Hebrew history angels were thought to be supernatural beings who were attendant to God. In the New Testament there are several references to hosts of angels as well as to single angels. Currently we often hear it said that some mysterious or unexplainable events must be the work of angels. At those times, we think of angels as being God's divine representatives who live among us and who function in any number of ways. We most often think of angels as messengers or guardians who are sent by God to protect or guide us. Some of us may feel more comfortable calling an angel the Holy Spirit whom we feel guides us and protects us through the still small voices of God deep within us.

Our grandson, Hart, has had a course in comparative religion this semester at the university which he is attending. In a recent conversation he and my husband were discussing angels. Hart said he has come to believe that guardian angels guide him and protect him every day.

Billy Graham felt the idea was important enough to write an entire book about angels. Some years ago, the contemporary Christian singer/songwriter Michael W. Smith recorded the song, "Emily," in which he speaks of an angel. One line of the song is: "You're an angel just waiting for your wings."

During this special season we are very much aware of the various ways and times that God comes into our lives. He sends events and individuals into our lives to enrich them. He sent Jesus Christ, His Son, into our lives to change them.

Think for a moment about those special individuals whom God has sent into your life this past year in ways that have been very meaningful to you.

- Perhaps it was a close family member—your husband or your wife, a parent, a child, whose counsel and love sustained you.
- Perhaps it was a doctor who enhanced the quality of your life through knowledge of medical science or skilled hands.
- Perhaps it was a friend who celebrated a special joy with you.
- Perhaps it was a minister or a Sunday school teacher whose insights inspired you and helped you grow in your faith.
- Perhaps it was a neighbor or a friend who came when you were grieving over the loss of a loved one.
- Perhaps it was your best friend who phoned you and brought cheer into your life on a "down day."

God does minister to us through others. That is one way He has chosen to make a difference in our lives almost every day. Perhaps you and I know some angels to whom we would say today, "You are an angel just waiting for your wings."

Out of the Darkness

The lives of God's chosen people, the Hebrews, had reached rock bottom. It was a time of severe economic, social, and even religious tension and unrest. The desperate conditions had spread out from Jerusalem, even to the little remote town called Nazareth, and to all points in between and beyond.

For too long the Jewish people had been living under the heavy heel of the Roman civil and military powers which ground them down. Heavy taxation had kept them poor. They were looked down upon as the "common people" of the land. To make matters more humiliating, Roman officials would find a Jew, one of their own number, who would serve as the tax collector and would collect the money from his own extended family, friends, and neighbors. This practice often led to graft and exploitation when the tax collector would collect more money than Rome required. He could skim the extra amount off the top in order to increase his pay. In general, these Jewish tax collectors were despised and hated by the Hebrew people.

A final blow came when a decree came from Rome requiring every Jewish man to travel to the city of his birth to register. We can easily see that this kind of tabulation would be a valuable tool for the Romans to use in a census count. The Roman government was concerned about the rapid growth in the number of Jews who lived in each province.

So it was into this kind of darkness that God chose to send His Son, not as a conquering king but as a harmless gift—a baby. A dear friend summed it up well in her Christmas letter when she wrote: "The darkness of Advent was pierced and lighted by God's love."

As I ponder Christ's birth I ask myself this question: "What if Jesus, the baby, had not come to become Jesus Christ the Man, our Savior?" Because He came two thousand years ago everything has been changed by those who have believed in Him. It has changed the kind of people we are, the way we live, and the way we treat each other.

A Christmas card from some other dear friends contained this provoking challenge:

> The best things to give this Christmas—
> to your enemy—forgiveness
> to your opponent—tolerance
> to your child—a good example
> to your parents—conduct to make them proud
> to yourself—respect
> to all people—charity and love.
>
> —Author Unknown

You and I may strive to give those gifts this Christmas if we welcome the baby of Bethlehem into our hearts as our Savior and Lord. This Christmas I am reminded of a prayer we used to sing when we sat around a campfire years ago:

> Into my heart, into my heart,
> Come into my heart, Lord Jesus.
> Come in today, come in to stay,
> Come into my heart, Lord Jesus.
> Amen.

A Fresh Start

A Fresh Start

And now let us welcome the New Year full of things that have never been.

—Rainer Maria Rilke

*O*ur gracious God has given us the gift of memory so that we may recall the many good things from the year we have just lived. God has also given us the gift of anticipation as we embrace the beginning of a new year.

In *The Timepiece,* Richard Paul Evans quotes from the diary of David Parkins, one of the main characters in the book. He says, "Sometimes I wish it were within my power to reach forth my hand and stop this moment, but to hold the note is to spoil the song! Life goes on, we cannot stop time." And so it moves on. We cannot stop it even though we may sometimes wish we could.

Someone has observed that time is like a snowflake. It disappears while we are trying to decide what to do with it. Everything that is the end of something is also the beginning of something new. At the end of the year we turn over a new page and start writing a new chapter at the beginning of this fresh untarnished new year.

I appreciate the writing of Molly Culbertson, the former editor of *Country Home* magazine. At the beginning of a new year she said she made only two New Year's resolutions instead of her accustomed long list. One of the resolutions was to complete several unfinished projects in her home and the second was to regularly give some volunteer time to a needy child.

At the end of the year she reported with a great deal of satisfaction that she had realized both resolutions.

Sometimes our lives seem so fragmented—so out of focus. Time does melt away like the snowflake in our hand and we have nothing to show for it. This year I have chosen one good thing to which I will give my best. Perhaps you would like to join me and select one good thing you would like to achieve. Joe E. Lewis once reminded his hearers: "You only live once, but if you work it right, once is enough."

The challenge of the prophet Isaiah is just as appropriate today as when he first wrote it centuries ago, "Forget the former things; see the 'new things' doing in our lives" (Isa. 43:18–19 NIV).

> Looking back may I be filled with gratitude;
> Looking forward may I be filled with hope;
> Looking upward may I be filled with strength;
> Looking inward may I be filled with peace.
>
>   —Author Unknown

Courage for Tomorrow Morning

When the wisemen followed a bright new star, they traveled into an unknown territory and into an unknown experience. Some astronomers believe the star was formed by a convergence of three major celestial bodies—Jupiter, Saturn, and Halley's Comet. Some say it was an early UFO. Others aren't sure what it was.

Most Biblical scholars believe the wisemen were Magi, who were learned scholars and Zoroastrian priests. They studied philosophy, theology, medicine, astrology, natural science, and religion. They probably came from an area which is now in Iran. Marco Polo told of visiting a small Persian village where he heard the legend that the wisemen had left from their village to follow the star. We do not know how many wisemen there were, but we have assumed that there were only three who made the journey because Matthew tells us they brought three costly gifts. Another tradition says that there were up to a dozen Magi from different countries who made the journey to Bethlehem. Some Biblical scholars say that they arrived in Bethlehem twelve days after the birth of Jesus when we celebrate Epiphany. Others believe that it was at least two months and possibly as long as two years before they found him. All scholars are agreed that Matthew was trying to tell his readers that God had sent Jesus to be king of the whole world and not only of the Jews.

In her book *Traveling Toward Sunrise*, Louise Haskins has described the courage and perseverance of these men from the East. She points out that their journey began about one thousand miles from Bethlehem. Then she writes:

These travelers were time's valiant great hearts. They were journeying on the star road making their way through an uninspiring land, a desert waste, upheld by hope of a glorious new day, a tomorrow morning, when with its darkness and shadows would be left far behind.

Travelers whose hopes were fixed on what was before and beyond; men of faith who followed the gleam loyally, right through to the very end; road-makers, presenting an unparalleled example of courage and bravery; men of vision, always looking ahead, never behind.

Each of us can relate to them as they journeyed into the unknown. For many of us, the fear of the unknown is one of our greatest anxieties.

The unfolding of every New Year takes each one of us on our own personal journey into the unknown. Many of us are looking for the Star which will guide us. Experience tells us that there will be many hours of joy and some hours of heartache; some hours of accomplishment and others when things will be left undone; new friends found and old friends lost. The book of Proverbs contains a promise I like to read at the beginning of each New Year: "In every thing you do, put God first and He will direct you and crown your efforts with success" (3:6 OLB).

The unknown minutes and months of the New Year are not given to us by God to squander or to fear; they have been loaned to us by God to use in loving service for Him and to others. He will give us the courage to face whatever each new day will bring. I was impressed by a statement in a recent written-for-television Christmas movie: "Courage is not the absence of fear; courage is taking action in the face of fear."

Once again, I am reminded of some very special words which Louise Haskins wrote when she described her journey into the unknown New Year:

> And I said to the man who stood at the gate of the year, "Give me a light that I might tread safely into the unknown!" And he replied, "Go out into the darkness and put your hand into the hand of God. That will be to you better than a known way."

So, I went forth, and finding the hand of God, trod gladly into the night.

Gifts That Last All Year

We are in the days of Epiphany, a time for pondering the wonders of Christmas. Christmas is a time of gifting when God gave His most precious gift, the one He loved so much, Jesus Christ, His Son.

I like to think God gave His gift to us with joy. He made the birth announcement, not to those who expected it most, but to the lowly unsuspecting shepherds. He told them of the Savior who had now come to them and to everyone in the whole world. God gave the first gift to us because He loves us. We continue giving to those whom we love in our families and among our friends. That gives us joy also.

You and I may have the joy of giving to others all year long. It can be Christmas every day of our fresh new year. How great that would be! Henri Nouwen, the well-known Dutch writer, has observed that our greatest joy and sense of fulfillment in life comes to us as we give to others. Here are some possible ways that we may give to each other this year. They are intangibles and do not require pretty gift bags with crushed tissue to hold them in place. They are the kind, thoughtful, and considerate gifts which we can all give to those about us.

- A pleasant smile and a happy facial expression as we meet and greet others will lighten and brighten their day.
- A "thank you" to others isn't expensive. When we say, "Thank you for helping me" to the clerk in the store or the nurse in the doctor's office who is tired after being on her feet all day we give her a lift.

- An attitude of "listening with our heart" when we are talking with someone shows that we really are interested and care about what they are saying.
- Our presence by just being there to hold a hand or give a friendly hug can give comfort when there is no need for words.
- Our time as we sit down to write a note to others which they may read at their convenience will let them know of our love and concern. This will cost us only a few cents, and I'm sure each of us can afford that.
- Our courtesy in every situtation is such a special gift.

For example, my husband and I stopped in a restaurant to eat after an afternoon of last-minute Christmas errands. The restaurant was packed with weary shoppers. A pleasant young man came promptly to take our order. We had a long wait for our food, but our waiter came back twice to apologize for the delay because the kitchen could not keep up with the orders. We assured him that we were enjoying our coffee while we relaxed a bit.

Meanwhile, a middle aged couple was seated in the booth next to ours. They also had to wait for their food. When the young man came to apologize to them for the delay, the man loudly and obnoxiously expressed his anger. Later, when the young man brought his food, the man verbally abused the waiter and sent the food back to the kitchen. When the waiter brought a second plate to him, he refused it also.

The manager came to his table and spoke quietly to the impatient customer, but the man was still very adamant. Such an unhappy and selfish man!

When the frustrated young waiter brought our check to us, we expressed our appreciation for his good service and tipped him generously. He smiled broadly as he thanked us and then he said, "You've made my day." A little courtesy goes a long way and may help when it's sorely needed.

- Our prayers can be our greatest gift to others.

We believe and know that our prayers for others do make a difference. God is faithful and will answer them in ways which are most beneficial to all. Our gifts of prayer for others will also bring to us what Henri Nouwen called our greatest sense of joy and fulfillment.

My New Year's resolution this year: I will try, with God's help, to generously share these and other gifts with all those whom I meet. Will you join me?

Selected Sources

Albom, Mitch. *Tuesdays with Morrie*. New York: Doubleday, 1997.

Baptismal Covenant, The United Methodist Book of Worship. Nashville: The United Methodist Publishing House, 1992.

Blanchard, Richard. *Fill My Cup, Lord*. United Methodist Hymnal, Nashville: United Methodist Publishing House, 1989.

Bonhoeffer, Dietrich. *Letters and Papers From Prison*, New York: Macmillian, 1972.

Bowring, John, (1825) *In the Cross of Christ I Glory*, United Methodist Hymnal. Nashville: United Methodist Publishing House, 1989.

Breathnach, Sarah Ban. *Simple Abundance*. New York: Warner Books, 1995.

———. *Something More: Excavating Your Authentic Self*. New York: Warner Books, 1998.

Carlson, Richard. *Don't Sweat the Small Stuff—and It's All Small Stuff*. New York: Hyperion, 1997.

Carroll, Lewis. *Through the Looking Glass*. New York: Maxwell Macmillan International, 1993.

Evans, Richard Paul. *The Timepiece*. New York: Simon and Shuster, 1996.

Fuller, Ethel Romig. "God Hears Prayer," 1000 Quotable Poems. Chicago: Willett Clark and Co., 1937.

Goethe, J. W. von. *Live Each Day*, 1000 Quotable Poems. Chicago: Willett Clark and Co., 1937.

Haskins, Louise. *Traveling Toward Sunrise*. Grand Rapids: Zondervan.

Lawrence, Brother. *Lord of All Pots and Pans*. Publisher Unknown.

Lindbergh, Ann Morrow. *Gift From the Sea*. New York: Pantheon Books, 1955.

Longfellow, Henry Wadsworth. *Too Late: World's Best Loved Poems*. New York: Harper and Bros., 1927.

Mother Theresa. *In My Own Words*. Liguori, Mo: Liguori Press, 1996.

Oxenham, John. *A Highway and a Low: Quotable Poem*. Chicago: Willett Clark and Co., 1937.

Quoist, Michel. "The Wire Fence" from *Prayers*. New York: Sheed and Ward, 1975.

Rilke, Rainer Marie. *Letters to a Young Poet*. New York: W. W. Norton, 1934.

Schopenhauer, Authur (1788–1860). *The Works of Schopenhauer*, abridged, edited by Will Durant. New York: Simon and Schuster, 1931.

Sleeth, Natalie. *Hymn of Promise*, United Methodist Hymnal. Nashville: The United Methodist Publishing House, 1989.

Stidger, William L. "I Saw God Wash the World," 1000 Quotable Poems, Chicago: Willett Clark and Co., 1937.

Studder-Kennedy, G. "Indifference," 1000 Quotable Poems. Chicago: Willett Clark and Co., 1937.

Swindoll, Charles. *Challenging Words*. Dallas: Word Publishing, 1994.

———. *The Finishing Touch*. Dallas: Word Publishing, 1994.

Tournier, Paul. *The Meaning of Gifts*. Translated by John S. Gilmour. Richmond: John Know Press, 1963.

Wells, Charles. *Dear Old Man*. Nashville: Backbone Press, 1995.

About the Author

$\mathcal{M}$ary Jane Hartman has an uncommon sensitivity to the beauty and spiritual messages of the ordinary. Her appreciation for life's gifts led her into a career of music and teaching, graduating from Westmar University in Le Mars, Iowa, with a degree in music education in 1945. Active in the Belle Meade and Brentwood United Methodist Churches in Tennessee, Hartman has locally been acknowledged as United Methodist Woman of the Year in 1996 and has served as a conference devotional leader and as a member of the Women's Division of the Board of Global Ministries. Hartman has previously written devotional meditations for other publications including *Images: Women in Transition*.

Mary Jane lives in Brentwood, Tennessee, with her husband of fifty-eight years, Warren Hartman. She has one daughter, Suzanne, and a special son-in-law, Don Knight. They live in Memphis. Mary Jane also has two grandchildren, Amy, a teacher, and Hart, a pre-law student.